THE KORE GODDESS
A Mythology and Psychology

THE KORE GODDESS
A Mythology and Psychology

SAFRON ROSSI

WINTER PRESS

AN IMPRINT OF
SPRING PUBLICATIONS

The Kore Goddess: A Mythology and Psychology

Published by Winter Press
Arroyo Grande, CA
www.winterpresspublishers.com

Winter Press is an imprint of Spring Publications
www.springpublications.com

Library of Congress Control Number: 2020924370
ISBN: 978-1-7362057-0-9

Second printing 2022

COPYRIGHT ACKNOWLEDGMENTS
Grateful acknowledgment is made for permission to reprint:
Poems by Sappho from *Sappho*, translated by Mary Barnard.
Reprinted with permission by University of California Press, 1986.
Quotes from the unpublished lecture transcript *The Power of the Maiden*
by Jane Hollister Wheelwright, 1984. Quoted with permission
from Betty Wheelwright.

Cover Design by Jonas Perez
Interior book design by Joanna Bizior

I shall be a
virgin always
Sappho

CONTENTS

Korai Triad Goddesses

To my beloved husband, Glen,
for his sagacious guidance,
support and encouragement
throughout this book's long gestation.
I am eternally grateful.

ILLUSTRATIONS

The author and publisher wish to thank the custodians of the artworks and photographs who granted permission for their use.

INTRODUCTION

Many years ago I stood beneath the night sky in the Black Rock Desert of Nevada. The seven sisters of the Pleiades constellation hung overhead and, as I thought about their story, a question descended, *Why are goddesses in Greek myth so often imagined in groups*? On the heels of this came, *What do mythic images of feminine plurality symbolize in the psyche*? These became the questions that inspired and organized my subsequent doctoral research on triad goddesses in Greek myth—the Fates, Furies, Graces, Hours, Sirens, Graiai, Thriai—and the relationship between these figures of feminine multiplicity and women's psyches.

Some years later it was in another nightscape where the key insight for this current work emerged. In the underground vault of the Opus Archives manuscript collections housed at Pacifica Graduate Institute I came across an unpublished lecture titled "The Power of the Maiden" (1984) by Jane Hollister Wheelwright. Her mythic amplification of the Maiden archetype led me to consider again the triad goddesses, who have in common the distinct attributes of being neither wife or mother. I realized then that notwithstanding the particular archetypal realties each triad personifies, they are also all Maiden, in Greek, *Kore* (pronounced kor-ray) goddesses. Just as one is startled when a shooting star streaks across

13

the sky, I suddenly recognized the Kore as the deeper pattern that both connected and animated the triad goddesses in an altogether different way than I had considered before. This insight launched my study of the Kore archetype and the mythic figures who personify its perspective and values. My early research and writing on the triads paved the way for the largely neglected theme of the Kore.

The Kore is the archetypal Virgin or Maiden, a youthful figure who is one-in-herself. To characterize such a figure as archetypal is to recognize its universality and timeless psychological value. This value is associated with psychological integrity. The Kore's virginity or unto-oneself fullness describes what it means to be grounded in one's essential nature as an individual. As the figure most directly concerned with our connection to the interior rhythms of our being, contact with this archetype brings a sense of sovereignty and potency.

While the idea of the individual has always been of singular importance in Western civilization, the psychological value of the Kore at this particular moment in the evolution of culture is increasingly crucial. The collective pressures of life have become unrelenting in our fast-paced technological world, which has both dark and light dimensions. In this Promethean realm, largely fueled by capitalism and the engine of social media, the inner life is exploited daily for profit. On the other hand, our greater connectivity makes us aware of the urgent need for social justice and political action both across town and the globe. For good or for ill, digital technology has been designed and is currently implemented in the social sphere to continually draw us out of ourselves. Another valence lies closer to home. Our worldview is initially shaped by our family and culture through the myriad of rules, mores, or 'shoulds' that denote principles we are taught to adopt as our own. To discover the values that align with our nature, in other words to be an individual, requires a withdrawal of the psychological investiture in the parental complexes at work in both the personal and collective dimensions. Whether this process brings us back to those inherited communal values or sends us off into foreign lands, what matters is that we come to know what really belongs to us. It is the Kore who personifies that force which compels us to resist outer influences and defend the integrity of our inner ground.

Thus we could say it is the function of the Kore to safeguard us from losing ourselves to collective forces by turning us inward. Shining a light on the psychological task both women and men now face, the Kore asks, *How do we make a place for ourselves, within ourselves, that is inviolable, virginal?*

The Kore-Virgin has been largely buried in the cultural imagination over the last two millennia. This has made the pattern of consciousness she personifies difficult to recognize and her gravitas profoundly undervalued. The aim of this book is to raise the Kore to her own standing among other primary feminine archetypes, and this will also work to raise our consciousness of a sphere of lived experience that has been overshadowed by those other archetypal figures, particularly the Mother and the Daughter. By gathering forgotten forms that express critical yet neglected modes of being, we broaden our understanding of the ways soul-making happens. This renewal of vision has to do with the arduous work of peeling away essential forms from social roles, so we can explore the Kore as a quality of consciousness rather than literal model of behavior.

My decision to use *Kore* rather than the more recognizable *Virgin* or *Maiden* is based in part on what I see as the need to rehabilitate our imagining into this archetypal mode of being through language. *Virgin* once carried sacred value because it meant a being or person possessing spiritual potency. Now understood solely in secular and literal terms, it indicates little more than one's sexual status. Novelist Ursula Le Guin sums up the situation: "the once awesome 'virgin' is now a sneer or at best a slightly dated word for a person who hasn't copulated yet."[1] Alternatively, *maiden* is conspicuously old fashioned conjuring ghosts of slightly mad (or mean) old aunts, or buxom bodice-bound milk-maids and barmaids. While Hollister Wheelwright excavates *maiden* to its Indo-European root of *mag,* which means 'to have power,' somehow the rehabilitation of this word feels awkward. Something fresh is required to recapture our imagination. *Kore,* a new but ancient word, helps cut through the heavy dross of the old cultural stereotypes, bringing us back in touch with something that is alien and yet deeply familiar.

While Kore-Virgins have been figures of profound spiritual power and significance that have appeared cross-culturally and at various times throughout history, the ancient Greek world provides us with some of the most recognizable and significant renderings of the type especially in the goddesses Persephone, Artemis, and Athena, and in the special grouping of archaic Kore statues which form the axis of this study. This leads to the second reason I have chosen the term *Kore*, for it not only indicates the mythic landscape this book inhabits but also underscores a primary idea of archetypal thought, namely the primacy of the Greek imagination in the Western psyche. "Turning within, we must see that *we are Greeks*," writes Ginette Paris, "and that this fact has nothing to do with the geography of our birth, nor with the epoch in which we live, but with our Occidental origins, since it is from ancient Greece that our civilization was born."[2] Acknowledging this does not take away the need for Western culture to recognize its shortcomings and biases. But even as multicultural persons, we are in a Western democracy and have Western ways of understanding human nature.

A re-connection to origins is necessary for any real renewal of the imagination. It is out of this psychic soil that the Kore reveals her root meanings of youthfulness, vitality and sovereignty. For the Greeks, to be kore or virgin did not mean being sexually chaste but *unmarried*, therefore undivided or in integrity with oneself. This understanding of the Kore returns us to a level of meaning that has been long obscured by Judeo-Christian influences which emphasize literal chastity and purity.

The third factor that contributed to my decision is the place the Kore is accorded by C. G. Jung. As will be discussed in chapter one, Jung recognized her foremost significance for women and placed her among the chief archetypes of psychic life. Esther Harding, Jane Hollister Wheelwright and Irene Claremont de Castillejo were Jungian analysts who took Jung's ideas on the Kore further and pushed them into a conversation on women's psyches and feminine images of the Self. To reestablish our connection to the life principles this figure personifies we also need to retrieve the insights from their groundbreaking work.

Framing this introduction within origin landscapes is about getting to those root factors that are intrinsic to shape and character. This brings us to the fundamental idea in Jungian and archetypal psychology about myth being the psyche's primary language. While specific myths arise out of a particular culture, shaped by the environment, history, language, ritual and arts of a people, they also deal with universal themes that are the shared inheritance of humanity, with which everyone can resonate or understand. As the most direct expression of the archetypal realm, myths reflect the structure and dynamics of psychological life. In our psyche-centered study of myth we are exploring the inner world that pervades and informs all outer life. Turning to these ancient tales, we become more conscious and capable of differentiating the archetypal realities that undergird and direct this life.

While myths describe the archetypal realities of life experiences, they are at the same time fictional stories whose origins are ultimately unknown. In essence, myths are stories that are true on the inside but untrue on the outside. This ambiguity is fundamental to the nature of myth and is what makes for the imaginal possibilities it engenders. As James Hillman succinctly puts it, "Myths do not ground, they open."[3] Myths are less like maps and more like impressionist paintings. They don't refer to our day world actions and how we ought to behave. Rather, they reveal symbolic realities that give us insight into the psychic spaces within which we find ourselves. By means of metaphor, myths express the enduring, fundamental, archetypal nature and imaginal reality of the soul.

The goddesses and gods of myth are the intelligible forms of the soul. They embody the psyche, which reveals itself through their actions, their mannerisms, their madnesses. This metaphorical perspective comes to us directly from the ancient Greeks. In the words of the pre-Socratic poet-philosopher Empedocles, a god "is not furnished with a human head upon his body; he has not arms…he has no feet, nor knees to run, nor hairy parts of generation. Rather he is a Mind, holy and ineffable, and that alone, flashing with swift thoughts throughout the whole order of the world."[4] That is to say, the goddesses and gods are to be understood as psychic movements that can flare through anyone and anything. They are not human, though their human form can make us forget this principal fact. As underlying constellations of consciousness, the gods shine a light upon our complexes, those inner and outer conflicts that shape the events of our lives. They personify what we long for, what we need, what we spend our lives seeking to experience. Our work, following Jung's principle of individuation and Hillman's notion of soul-making, is to cultivate a quality of consciousness that sees life itself in mythic terms, where we open into deeper imaginings and ways to story our experience.

A further important idea to note about myth is its complexity. While we may be familiar with one telling of a particular story, scratch the surface of these protean tales and other accounts will appear. That there are often many versions means there is no one true or real story. This is consonant with the variety of interpretations myth engenders, which challenge, support, complicate, and deepen one another. Like the many colored panes of stained glass that form a cathedral rose window, a myth is all of its variants, every pane providing another color or perspective, while each interpretation is like a ray of light reflecting our understanding for the complexity of myth and, ultimately, of the psyche.

An archetypal study requires having an eye for polytheistic interactions among archetypal figures and an understanding of psychological maturation. Jung's idea of individuation points us to the telos or ultimate aim of the soul and encourages the search for language that describes the larger ordering intelligence that vessels soulful experience. Hillman opens up the psyche's mythopoetic world through the mythic figures with an emphasis on the specificity of images. Both these approaches inspire and inform my work. As a figure of poise, sovereignty, and integrity, the Kore embodies the inner gravity of Jung's notion of the Self, and as a movement of consciousness evident in many goddesses, the Kore also draws us into Hillman's emphasis on the particular—the 'who' or 'what'—that is displayed in the psyche's imaginings.

Another place where I weave between the Jungian and archetypal approaches is in regards to gender. In writing about the Kore, I am following the Jungian understanding that there are feminine and masculine dimensions in the psyches of both women and men. As archetypal patterns, which is how Jung described feminine and masculine, they are psychic principles or qualitative energies in nature that are unknowable in themselves and therefore discernible only in symbolic forms and mythic images. As root metaphors for the energies of the psyche, they are naturally somewhat shaped by biological realities and experiences of female and male sex. While this is what has partly informed cultural gender ideas of woman and man, these principles are not bound or limited to physical or social forms of expression. By definition, what is archetypal is universal, accessible to all persons. The archetypes per se are fluid and unfixed, capable of numerous manifestations that bespeak changing psychic realities that characterize individual and collective experience.

My approach is to strike a fidelity to the mythic image, which is one of the key principles of archetypal psychology. To stay with the image means working directly with the figures as they present themselves in their qualitative specificity. Where feminine and masculine easily become abstractions, and are often discussed in Jungian thought as hypostases, attentive discernment of the image keeps us grounded in the phenomenological language of the psyche. Jules Cashford's description of how this looks is helpful, "imaginatively, we are *all* Gilgamesh…*all* Odysseus going home *and* Penelope at the loom…The poetic image, like the universal dimension of myth, is beyond gender."[5] In so far as possible this is the way I try to move as this approach emphasizes the specificity and complexity of the mythic images and the psychological resonances at work, to different degrees, in all of us. Nonetheless, in order to remain conversant with classical Jungian discourse, I will at times lean on the feminine and masculine distinction. In all instances they are to be understood in archetypal rather than social terms.

To the extent that women's psychology appears more profoundly affected by the Kore pattern, this book does have a special relationship to women. The study offers an archetypal background to aspects of women's experience that have been commonly devalued and denied. Western culture has by and large rejected women's unto-oneselfness, which Paris identifies in the "oblivion to which the Artemis archetype has been consigned by the fact that, in our culture, femininity is usually judged as a function of its value relative to man, child, or to society and that it is rarely honored in itself."[6] Because the Kore belongs to herself first and foremost, she challenges those paradigms wherein women are affirmed, and measured, by their connection and service to others. The absence of these Kore-Virgin values is what makes it, Paris continues, "difficult for girls and women to know, within themselves, that aspect of femininity which is not in relation to some other reality."[7] In a similar vein, Nor Hall writes in *The Moon and the Virgin* about the inner meeting that women must make in order to heal wounds whose medicine is not to be found in union with masculine consciousness. This healing by "an internal conjunction, by an integration of its own parts"[8] is bringing back together what has been torn apart in the imaginal bodies of feminine being and knowing. Among those figures who are crucial to this inner meeting is the Kore, for she is the one most directly concerned with the sanctity of inner life.

The Kore's reappearance is one critical response to the long repression of many facets of feminine consciousness, which has been enacted outwardly in the historical control and suppression of women. Such an archetypal response is related to the need to reclaim something that is deep and necessary to the soul. A parallel can be found in the middle of the last century in Jung's writing about the Assumption of Mary. The recognition of the divinity of the mother of God, which the ecclesiastical authorities hesitated to enact as official Church dogma, reflected the demand of the Catholic masses. Jung writes how "their insistence is, at bottom, the urge of the archetype to realize itself."[9] Cultural movements sometimes reveal shifts within the psyche that are in conflict with the structures and ideologies of society. The insistence by women over the last two centuries on their emancipation from second class status and their equal rights in all areas of citizenship can be understood as the urge of the Kore archetype to realize itself. It is in this spirit that I offer this work as a contribution to what Paris calls "imaginative feminism,"[10] which seeks to connect soul and social responses to both inner and outer situations. This polytheistic approach acknowledges the complexity of women's lived experience which cannot and should not be circumscribed by any one definition of feminism. Imaginative or archetypal feminism allows us to imagine each goddess as a constellation of light whose appearance in life invokes a world of concerns based on intrinsic values. To see each goddess as a face of feminism allows for both diversity and inclusiveness.

The book is arranged in three parts. The chapters that comprise Part I establish the essential understanding of the Kore as personifying that aspect of the psyche that has to do with the deep ground of character. Sovereign and one-in-herself, Kore-Virgin goddesses deal with this sense of being that is integral to all women. After a review of the origins of the Kore archetype in Jungian studies, the subsequent chapters are arranged around the phenomenology of the Greek archaic Kore statues which provide three focal themes that belong to this archetypal pattern: individuality, contained integrity, and spirited agency. These themes are amplified through Greek myth, literature, legendary women's histories, and depth psychological ideas on women's psyches. Part II deals with how the reemergence of Kore consciousness requires identification of one of the main barriers that have occluded this archetype, which is the Great Mother. The essential aspects of the Great Mother archetype, the special difficulties the Kore encounters in the realm of the Mother, and differentiation of the Kore and the Daughter are all discussed. Part III continues the archetypal study by looking at the special grouping of Korai (plural for Kore, pronounced kor-eye) triad goddesses and where we experience them in life. The Fates, Furies, Graiai, Graces, Hours, Sirens, and Thriai, and the archetypal values these triads personify amplify the Kore in surprising ways.

Lastly a note about terms—throughout the book archetypes are capitalized in order to distinguish between the universal and personal levels of experience, for example, archetypal Mother and personal 'mother'.

The Kore
Archetype

—

CHAPTER ONE

The Kore Archetype: Origins

Take a walk through any ancient Greek temple and you will see the Kore. She is that beautiful, youthful figure who stands with one foot slightly ahead of the other, dressed in intricately folded robes. She is graceful and has an attentive demeanor. She's often smiling. At the Acropolis of Athens, Korai once stood along the Erechtheion and Parthenon temples. The figures that still grace the Erechtheion, called the Carytids, evoke a sense of the presence Korai once commanded. At Hera's Temple on the island of Samos, Korai ringed her altar and lined the streets, marking the boundary of the temple ground. At Apollo's sanctuary in Didyma on the coast of Ionia in present-day Turkey, Korai surrounded his altar, and on the pediment at the temple of Apollo in Delphi on Mt. Parnassus in Greece, they flank him. Many of the ancient temples had terraces that displayed gifts to the gods, and Korai statues were always among them. In Kyrene, in what today is Libya, Korai once stood in the temples of Apollo, Artemis, and the Demeter sanctuary. In rural and cosmopolitan sanctuaries alike, the Kore has been found all across the ancient Mediterranean world.

"Greek religion," classicist Karl Kerényi confirms, "like no other the world over, is characterized by maiden Goddesses, indeed more markedly so than by the acknowledged lordship of Zeus over Gods and men," and never became "exclusively patriarchal."[11] Beyond the Kore figures that were paramount on temple grounds, Athena, Artemis, and Hestia are themselves all Kore goddesses, as well as Persephone who was *the* Kore goddess of the classical Greek world worshipped in the widespread Eleusinian mystery cult. And there are numerous other divinities, nymphs and mortals in Greek myth that are regarded as Kore, including the triad sister goddesses such as the Fates, Furies, and Graces to which I will turn later in this book.

C. G. Jung's extensive study of archetypes of feminine consciousness led him to the Kore, whom he all but identifies with the central archetype of the Self, or what he refers to as the "supraordinate personality."[12] The Self in Jung's thinking is that which moves a woman or man to a greater sense of their ensouled being. It can also be understood as the archetype of the whole. This principal significance of the Kore in women's psyches caused Jung to place this figure among his list of primary archetypes, along with the Shadow, Wise Old Man, Child, Mother, and the Anima and Animus.[13] And yet, even in circles of Jungian thought, this pattern is often overlooked.

It is the confluence of the extraordinary role of the Kore in ancient Greek cultural and religious vision and the significance of the Kore archetype in Jung's psychology that forms the premise of this study. If these figures were so prominent in the Greek imagination, and scholars in many fields, particularly depth psychology, have turned to that imagination as a template for Western consciousness, then what happened to this particular archetypal pattern? Despite the Kore's significance, there's a paucity of writing devoted to her. This work is my response to this insufficiency and to the obscuring of the archetype in the Western cultural imagination. It aims to show how the Kore personifies values that are deep, intrinsic, and necessary to the soul—sovereignty, individuality, vitality, youthfulness, and containment. Jung's writing on the Kore and the development of his ideas by Esther Harding, Jane Hollister Wheelwright and Irene Claremont de Castillejo on this figure's significance in women's psyches, is our starting point.

***

Jung wrote about feminine consciousness in a pervasive way and underscored its significance as an archetypal pattern that compensates the overly masculine orientation of Western culture, and he was the first to recognize the Kore's psychological significance. His treatment of this figure is limited to one essay, "On the Psychological Aspects of the Kore," which was originally published as a monograph alongside a piece by Kerényi on the Kore in Greek and Indonesian myth.[14]

In this groundbreaking essay Jung discusses how, as an expression of the archetype of the Self for women, the Kore has a power equivalent to that of the Mother in their psychology. While it can present as an entity, an image of the divinity living in a person's soul, the Self is also a dynamic process. Understanding it as a psychic movement is essential, as this is what drives individuation or the conscious realization of the whole of the personality, which includes unconscious as well as conscious components.[15] As this process joins the unconscious and conscious aspects of being, the Self also signifies the progress towards psychic integrity. As Aniela Jaffé describes it, the Self is "the immeasurable expanse of the psyche and at the same time its innermost core."[16] As a Self figure, the Kore therefore personifies this same psychic movement as well as the numinous potential of the conscious relation to one's own totality.

Jung describes how in myths, dreams, and active imaginations this archetypal figure appears as an unknown young girl, dancer, corybant (dancing celebrant of the goddess Cybele), maenad (a worshipper of Dionysus), or nymph.[17] He notes the Kore's peculiarity and that "the maiden is often described as not altogether human in the usual sense; she is either of unknown or peculiar origin, or she looks strange or undergoes strange experiences, from which one is forced to infer the maiden's extraordinary, myth-like nature."[18] After his descriptions of this unusual, beguiling figure and her psychological significance to women, Jung turns to focus on the Earth Mother and the Kore as an anima figure which in turn positions her role in the psychology of men.

Some years before Jung published this essay on the Kore, he was engaged in the *Visions Seminar*, a long series devoted to the imaginal

material of his analysand Christiana Morgan. In the course of psychologically amplifying the myth of Andromeda and Perseus in the 1932 Spring
term of the Seminar, Jung notes how the sacrifice of a beautiful young
woman is a common mythic motif and asks of the group, "What is this
beautiful daughter?" to which the analyst Barbara Hannah replies, "the
Self." One can imagine Jung's rejoinder as lightning quick, "Why should
that be a beautiful girl? I am quite certain that *my* Self is not a beautiful
girl."[19] Indeed. Although Hannah's response may have been tangential
to Jung's point, his response also seems to miss the mark. It sounds
true for Hannah and perhaps even relevant for Morgan whose fantasy
material Jung was discussing. It seems entirely possible this exchange
with a close colleague, as well as the insights he undoubtedly gathered
over the subsequent years, contributed to his later thoughts on the Kore
as a Self figure.

Both the idea of the Kore as a Self figure and the notion her power
is equivalent to that of the Mother are nearly unknown in depth psychological literature. As such a principal archetypal figure in women's
psyches, it seems incongruent that the Kore has been discussed so little.
In the index for Jung's *Collected Works,* under "kore" there are 9 entries whereas there are *three and a half pages* for "mother." Only a few
analysts and scholars have made in-depth studies of this figure and
her psychological significance, and the handful of works that do so are
either essays, comprise small sections of larger works, or remain unpublished. Another example of its absence is Claire Douglas's *The Woman
in the Mirror* (1990) which provides an excellent review of writing on
feminine archetypes and women's psychology by Jungian analysts up to
that point. There are no index entries for maiden, kore, or virgin. Kore
is not included as an archetype, despite Jung's inclusion of it in his list
of primary archetypes, as I noted. One must go to "daughter" which is
nested under "mother" and from there to "Kore/Persephone" located
under "Demeter." My drawing attention to this oversight is not so much
a commentary on Douglas's work per se but on what has not appeared
in the field at large. When the Kore's supreme psychological significance
is coupled with her near invisibility, it suggests there is something of the
Kore that courts paradox.

✶✶✶

In Greek, *kore* (κόρη), comes from the root for "vital force" as the principle which makes life grow.[20] Let's imagine this vital force in poet Dylan Thomas's terms as, "the force that through the green fuse drives the flower."[21] Though the Kore is most often depicted as a young woman, the word connotes youthfulness, not a particular number of years. We learn from the ancient tragedian Aeschylus, who called the three Graiai ancient maidens, *dênaiai korai,* that one can be aged and Kore; their grey hair crowns beautiful, youthful cheeks.[22]

There is a curious feature in the birth stories of Kore goddesses in Greek myth, for unlike Zeus, Hermes, and Dionysus who are born as babies, the Kore always takes her first breath immediately as a young woman—Athena springs from her father's head full-grown, Artemis is born a young girl immediately serving as midwife to her mother, and we first meet Persephone as a blossoming maiden in the fields. Not only does this 'just so' mythic phenomenon convey the profound significance of the Kore in Greek religion but also its archetypal gravity.

While the Kore may be generally unknown, her associate—the Virgin—is immediately recognizable. Synonymous with *kore* is *parthenos* (παρθένος), virgin or maiden, which denotes a woman who is unwed.[23] Both Kore and Parthenos are found in Greek literature and religion as epithets of many goddesses, most often translated simply as Virgin goddess. Let's consider virginity as the very broad archetypal stream from which more specific figures have emerged across time and cultures. There is mysterious Corn Maiden of Native American tradition, compassionate Christian Virgin Mother Mary, and fierce Nordic goddess Gefjun. In any mythic tradition there can be many Virgin goddesses, and this gives rise to further differentiations. In Greek myth, while the Amazon and the Kore spring from the same virginal river, they are not at all the same, as the Amazon's vigorous physicality expresses an extraversion that is not present in the Kore. And while Kore and Parthenos are often used synonymously, they are not simply equivalent, as Kore suggests something of the *essential vital force* that is particular to each person, whether she is a goddess or a mortal.

Some may find disquieting the fluidity that characterizes these various figures and their relative positions in the larger pattern. This is a problem of mythic territory, for there is an inherent difficulty in attempting to draw distinct boundaries around archetypal characters. The nature of the problem was stated by Jung in terms of not knowing the archetype as such, but only the cultural images that point to a hidden source, "One must constantly bear in mind that what we mean by 'archetype' is in itself irrepresentable, but that it has effects which enable us to visualize it, namely, the archetypal images."[24] Since we cannot put our finger on the archetype, we cannot draw clear boundaries around it. This means we're bound to find overlapping imagery and significant differences. Jung explains how because these conditions belong to the nature of archetypes,

> they can only be roughly circumscribed at best. Their living meaning comes out more from their presentation as a whole than from a single formulation. Every attempt to focus them more sharply is immediately punished by the intangible core of meaning losing its luminosity. No archetype can be reduced to a simple formula. It is a vessel which we can never empty, and never fill. It has a potential existence only, and when it takes shape in matter it is no longer what it was. It persists throughout the ages and requires interpreting ever anew. The archetypes are the imperishable elements of the unconscious, but they change their shape continually.[25]

The qualities of the broad archetypal stream of the Virgin were first brought to light in Esther Harding's *Woman's Mysteries: Ancient and Modern*, and a review of the principal features aids in identifying and drawing forth the Kore. The key element is Harding's translation of the Greek *parthenia* as unto-one-self, which expresses the inviolable essence of the Kore-Virgin archetype. This unto-one-selfness is the inner psychological reality expressed by the sovereignty that characterizes Virgin goddesses. While Harding does not name it as such, it is the Kore archetype she describes in the psychological meaning of the Virgin as undivided and unto-herself. She writes, "The characteristics of these great and powerful goddesses do not mirror those of any of the male gods, their histories are independent and the functions, their insignia and their rites being to themselves alone…They do not represent the feminine counterpart of characteristics originally male; they represent on the contrary the essence of the feminine in its sharpest contrast to the essence of masculinity."[26] We therefore find Virgin goddesses figuring in mythologies that are pre-patriarchal in their psychology, wherein feminine and masculine energies are distinctly different and coequal.

These expressions of the active power and independence of the Virgin crystallize the authority she symbolizes. Like the goddesses who bear their divinity in their own right, the woman who is psychologically Virgin, Harding writes, "is one-in-herself, [and] does what she does not because of any desire to please, not to be liked, or to be approved, even by herself; not because of any desire to gain power over another…but because what she does is true."[27] That is to say, the woman who is Virgin does not please even herself—in the egoic sense—for what she does is authentic to a deeper sense of self. This connection to her psychic depths is the result of being open to and in conscious relationship with the archetypal energies that shape and direct her life. Here we encounter one of the paradoxical aspects of the style of consciousness the Kore personifies, for she is simultaneously unto-herself and receptive. This receptivity to the inner world, whether in the vales of the soul or the heights of the spirit, is the source of Kore sovereignty.

While the Kore-Virgin is open to the energies of the interior realm, she is defended against outer expectations. To be unto-one-self means psychological sovereignty or living in alignment with one's deeper nature. This naturally stands in opposition to living solely along the traditional paths approved by the collective. Harding discusses how socially sanctioned expectations have led many women to live their lives in service to others rather than themselves. In contrast to this she writes, "One-in-herself, the woman who is psychologically virgin does not use her instincts or psychological energy to gain for herself that which denotes security in a patriarchal culture—husband, home and family."[28] Harding is making a crucial point about where and to what ends a woman directs her life energy. For the woman who is psychologically virgin, it is a transpersonal necessity to dedicate some measure of her vital energies to the discovery and affirmation of her self separate from her relationship to others and the sense of identity that comes from those areas of her life. This does not mean that a woman who is a wife and/or a mother cannot be psychologically virgin, but that she does not channel all of herself into her partner or children.

In many mythologies Virgin goddesses are also lunar goddesses, thus the ancient symbolism of the moon is a central theme of Harding's study. The deeper symbolism of the moon is profound if unknown to most. In its monthly emergence, illumination and disappearance, the moon instructs us about qualities of time and its cycles. The new moon heralds beginnings, the full moon drawing out the light of action, while the waning moon's decrease signals release and conclusions, and out of the darkness new life emerges again. These are the rhythms of change that underly all nature, for all things are born, mature, decline, and renew. The moon also teaches us how change happens slowly and deliberately. Understood metaphorically, the moon's phases mirror the inner world of emotions and psychological change, which likewise occur gradually and cyclically. When we are attuned to the moon we understand the recurring nature of our life energy—that periods of brightness and energy, as well as periods of darkness and heaviness, are natural. We also learn about engaging life with deliberation, reflection and patience. Thus for Harding, "the ancient religions of the moon goddess represent the education of the emotional life taking place not through a course or study, not even as the result of a system of discipline, though both these things doubtless entered in, but through an initiation."[29] These ancient lunar mysteries find their modern equivalents in our psychological lives for we too require meaningful initiation into the cyclic rhythms that shape and direct our emotions and relationships.

The Babylonian moon goddess Ishtar embodies the lunar cycle for she has both a life-giving waxing face and a death-bringing waning face. "She is the bright moon that rises as a tiny crescent in the sky, and night by night increases to fulness; and she is also the dark moon that creeps upon the full moon and eats it piecemeal, finally destroying it utterly."[30] In the mythos of Ishtar, the cyclic rhythm of the lunar month is inflected

Godden; Ishtar

in the seasonal rhythm of the year as whole. Tammuz, her lover-son, symbolizes earth's vegetal life and she puts him to death each year in the heat of the sun at the summer solstice. Mourning his loss, Ishtar descends into the underworld in order to bring him back. Her disappearance is a cause for mourning, and this period correlates with the seasonal dormancy of the soil. Upon her return with Tammuz from the realm of the dead, the earth comes to life again. In this part of the cycle, Ishtar's powers of sexuality and desire become paramount as the "awakener of the sexual impulse in animals and in men."[31] Her presence in the upper world ensure fecundity and increase in all life, while her absence means its decrease and barrenness. While her myth accords with the natural cycles of the earth's seasons and the propagation of crops, it is also reflective of the cyclic rhythms of psychic energy. The period of mourning that marks Ishtar's time in the underworld is akin to any period where there is an absence of vitality or libido, whereas her return is the renewal of the life force that naturally leads to activity and interest. Ishtar personifies the forces of life that mark these cycles, and the religious practices that surrounded her were ritualized expressions of these rhythms of inner and outer nature.

In other mythic traditions the Virgin moon goddess is one of three figures who together are the triple moon goddess, a universal personification of the three phases of the moon: the new moon Virgin, the full Moon Mother, and the waning, dark moon Crone. As a celestial symbol of feminine life energies, the moon reflects the dynamic process of becoming and the Virgin, Mother, and Crone have often been regarded as symbolizing stages of a woman's life. While the biological analogies are an important valence, these three figures are more than markers of time. Personifying qualities of consciousness, they have to do with life values and perspectives. So long as women do not identify with only one of these faces, all three are available and indeed may exist simultaneously. Full moon Mother consciousness is attentive to what needs nurturing. Concerned with making things thrive, keeping the ground fertile and creative, this Mother principle can apply to many areas of life, such as the development of a career or the nurturing of long-held dreams. One of the most direct encounters we can have with the full moon Mother aspect of ourselves is in our self care. When we are worn out from the demands of our busy lives, she invites us into her lap to rest (a nap, a hot bath, a walk along the ocean) without any judgement about what we have or have not accomplished.

Nothing is more entrancing than the full moon, but we know where there is great light there is an equally deep shadow, and those sides of the lunar feminine that belong to the dark have been mostly demonized, disregarded, and devalued. The Crone personifies the waning moon whose diminishing light leads to a merging with the darkness that envelops her. As the one who has matured through time and knows what has come to pass, this old woman has the long view. From flourishing to diminishment, and ultimately the relinquishment that death requires, the Crone is midwife to life's passages. Attuned to endings, she seeks out the right blessings to ease the transition to the other shore. Of the three moon goddesses, it is she who recognizes that what dies will become part of the nutrient-rich soil necessary for new life. These issues that belong to Crone territory—maturity, endings, and silence—are what we meet throughout life, not only in terms of physical aging and the passage of time. As we mature psychologically, old attitudes become untenable and require a kind of death. The Crone knows how to cut the psychic umbilical cords to help us come into our own. Often life is described as having phases, and whether the actions that bring a chapter to close occur swiftly or gradually, all eventually conclude and our attunement to Crone consciousness has to do with how we negotiate and meaningfully handle endings.

Much like how the entire circumference of the moon is often faintly visible throughout her phases, when taken together, the three faces of the triple moon goddess suggests a consciousness wherein all parts are seen to belong—Virgin new, Mother full, Crone veiled—as well as light and dark aspects. To feminine lunar consciousness, all phases and all parts belong to the whole, and this valuing of the integrity of the psyche means the contradictory parts of oneself are neither cut off or denied. This ancient image of feminine plurality, cyclic rhythms, and mutability contained in the wholeness of the moon is essential to the lunar archetype.

Harding's study of the Virgin moon goddesses provides critical mythic, as well as further psychological, amplification of Jung's initial insights about the Kore as a Self figure for women. Jane Hollister Wheelwright and Irene Claremont De Castillejo are two other first generation Jungian analysts who took Jung's ideas on the Kore and pushed them into a conversation about an emerging feminine god-image. Their writing explores in different ways how the Kore, who they call the Virgin or Maiden, are Self figures for women, imaginal persons who personify a sense of wholeness, meaning and guidance. Based on their psychoanalytic practices, their own inner work, and the societal shifts of the twentieth century, they were expanding Jung's contrasexual model of soul figures as it pertained to women's psyches and exploring issues around the Self and feminine images in the modern world.

In her unpublished lecture "The Power of the Maiden" (1984), Hollister Wheelwright shares how her work with female analysands between the 1960s and 1980s, those pivotal decades of the second wave women's movement in the US, led her to identify how the female unconscious was gravitating toward the Maiden, who was a "more ageless, more ideal and mysterious figure of the female aspect of the Self than the Old Earth Mother who, because of patriarchal domination, became less comprehensive."[32] Whereas at one time the Mother was the ideal image of woman's psychic totality, this appears to be changing with the emergent Kore-Maiden now reflecting more fully the complexity of women's beingness. A new valence is becoming visible, one that Hollister Wheelwright sees as reflective of the changes women are undergoing personally.

Hollister Wheelwright's archetypal Maiden, which she traces to the Indo-European root *mag*, "to have power," is unmarried—an independent Virgin who embodies the qualities of "uniqueness, youth, power, [is] changeable like the moon, [a] personification of nature."[33] Among the mythic figures Hollister Wheelwright draws upon to amplify the archetype are the Sumerian sister goddesses Inanna and Ereshkigal. She discusses how the erotic poems of Inanna express an earthiness and ribaldry that is associated with the Maiden's powers, and the mysteries of initiation and transformation that belong to Ereshkigal's realm show a dark chthonic aspect of this earthiness.[34] She identifies in the Old Testament Eve the Maiden's youthful spirit of adventure. These various qualities lead Hollister Wheelwright to conclude that this archetype is multivalent, appearing as a "composite of daughter, sister, young mother, virgin, goddess, prostitute, psychopomp, priestess and more,"[35] and as such it is a pattern of consciousness that provides a more inclusive model of the female unconscious. This combination of virginity and multivalence (*valentia* means vigor, strength or capacity) echoes the triple moon goddesses whose multiplicity is contained in a unity. The emergence of the Maiden is therefore indicative of the deeper psychic shifts occurring in women which is leading to the recognition that there are many aspects to their nature.

The plurality of the Kore and her resonance in the female psyche is the theme of Irene Claremont De Castillejo's profound essay "Soul Images of Women," which explores the question of how women visualize their souls.[36] Based on deep engagement with her analysands as well as her own dreams and active imaginations, De Castillejo understands *women's innermost soul figures are feminine.* This radical insight establishes two things. First, it marks a shift away from Jung's view of the contrasexual dynamics of the psyche, which he theorized that since for a man his soul or anima is personified as a feminine figure, the inverse would be the case for women. Second, it validates Jung's brief but potent thesis that the Kore is a Self figure for women. In De Castillejo's case study illustrations of feminine soul figures, all the examples pertain to a maiden or young girl. While unnamed as such, the Kore can nevertheless be recognized as the organizing force of the essay.

De Castillejo does not amplify the Maiden through myths or fairytales, rather she provides life sketches from her analytical practice. In the case of dreams, she discusses how the female soul figure often appears in the form of a young girl who can be the dreamer's companion appearing immediately at her side, or she may be a figure encountered elsewhere in the dreamscape. Sometimes a father figure leads the dreamer to a young girl. In these instances, De Castillejo notes how it is the animus, the masculine aspect of the woman's psyche, who acts as a psychopomp or guide to the soul figure rather than being that figure themselves. Some dreams she shows it is the inverse, as in one example the dreamer is led up to an attic by a young girl and there she finds a well-known male, whom the dreamer identifies as her animus, kneeling on the floor in prayer. De Castillejo understands the young girl who leads the dreamer to be her own soul figure before "it got overlaid with a masculine education and hidden out of sight."[37] She goes on to note that as this analysand continued working with her dreams and became more aware and related to this inner, young girl, "this figure grew up and now appears an ageless but very feminine woman."[38] These striking qualities of agelessness and femininity belong to the Kore.

One particular active imagination by De Castillejo's analysand, Jane, provides a most impressive illustration of the Kore as a Self figure. It was night, and being pursued by a group of men, Jane entered a large house surrounded by a moat. She walked into a room where the only light was from a large fireplace, beside which sat an old woman and a young girl. The old woman told Jane not to worry about the men, that they couldn't see despite the moonlight and that they would soon fall into the moat. She then beckoned Jane to play a game of draughts (checkers) with her, in the course of which "the old woman contrived that Jane should win, seemingly playing the white draughts as well as her own, though it was Jane's hands which moved them."[39] As they played, Jane noticed that the young girl was growing larger, and though she stood by the fire, her hair was wet as if she had just come out of the sea. Three silver fish leapt out of the girl's mouth and into the fire where they turned red gold as they swam among the flames. The girl then caught the fish and swallowed them, her white neck turning rosy warm in hue. The light from the fish in the girl's belly illuminated the space and Jane could see beautiful wall paintings and fine art objects in the room. The girl then went outside and because her light was stronger than the cold moonlight, the flowers in the garden were illuminated as she walked by them. She then dove into the moat.

De Castillejo's interprets the house surrounded by a moat as symbolic of the Self, and the figure that occupies the center of this Self symbol is not an old man but a *wise old woman*. Furthermore, she notes that the old woman configures things so that Jane should win in their game illustrates not only the excellent relationship between the ego and the Self, but also how the Self is an organizing power. This power is not a static entity but a movement, as in the psyche is 'Self-ing,' which we could imagine as our awareness becoming more particular and more sensitive to the presence of this organizing power that personifies those ultimate values that make life meaningful.

The wise old woman however is not alone in the house, there is the strange young girl seated beside the fire. Appearing as both old woman and as young girl, the feminine Self displays its infinite variety, underscoring the multivalent nature of the Kore archetype. This is also an illustration of the aged youthfulness that Aeschylus attributed to the Kore. I have come to understand this pairing of the old woman and young girl as an expression of the paradox of old and young, and how endings and beginnings, as well as the many different roles our lives require, can be more consciously engaged when one has that sense of being in touch with the source of one's depth or Virgin nature. In the same way that Jung defined the Self as both center and circumference of the psyche, the Kore is also a paradox that stands for the ability woman has to inhabit the various aspects of her being out of a creative center.

When gathered together, Harding, Wheelwright and De Castillejo's understandings of the Kore-Virgin archetype presents a figure of extraordinary power and deep significance. While each treats this pattern, its symbolic qualities, and its appearance in life in distinct ways, their studies make evident two outstanding and consistent features. First and foremost each writer emphasizes the sovereignty or one-in-herself essence. The second feature that emerges as a vital feature of this archetype's phenomenology is multivalence. Harding's elucidation of the Virgin moon goddesses and their simultaneously plural yet whole and undivided nature established these paradoxical aspects of the Kore-Virgin, which De Castillejo and Hollister Wheelwright have also shown to be at work.

CHAPTER TWO

Archaic Korai Statues

The Kore expresses the differentiation and cultural manifestation of the Virgin archetype in the Greek imagination, setting her apart from other figures that participate in the broader pattern. While this archetype is observable in the Kore goddesses of the Olympian pantheon, as well as in the other mythic figures Harding, Hollister Wheelwright, Jung and Kerényi compared in their essays, I want to begin with something that is arguably more essential and close to the core of the archetypal pattern. To understand the essential vitality and sovereignty that animates the Kore, we have turn to her iconography in archaic Greek statues.

In Greece, light penetrates everything. On the Acropolis in Athens, both the specter of Greece's ancient glory and the sweltering sun reflecting off the white marble ruins are awe-inspiring. The vast implacable presence of the sky, eternal Mediterranean blue, gleams. Gazing up past the bleached marble columns that seem to strive up toward luminosity, one feels the Titan Ouranos's groaning weight pressing down, as if these ancient temples are what created the space for life between heaven and earth. On this sacred hill, shadows are but variations of bending light. This assures the Acropolis its status as sacrosanct to Athena Glaukopis, bright-eyed goddess.

Below the hilltop temple to the south is the Acropolis Museum, and though the central hall is lightfilled, it is windowless and cool, providing respite from the blazing sun. The glass floor ripples, transparent frames revealing excavated remnants of the city beneath one's feet. On display in the Gallery of the Slopes of the Acropolis are fragments from the small sanctuaries that were constructed along the hill up to Athena's temple. The *steles* (inscribed stone slabs), vases, sculptures, and other votive or gift offerings had all been created for religious purposes, whether in worship of the divinity, in memory of a deceased family member, or to display a nation's wealth thereby affirming Athena or Zeus's beneficence. It was there that I understood with newfound clarity how the religious belief that marked the Greek imagination was an expression of their reverence for life. In Greek religion, everything truly essential was regarded as holy, and this expression of divinity in life made for a unique combination of worldliness and naturalness. Classicist Walter Otto explains: "In their world the divine is not superimposed as a sovereign power over natural events; it is revealed in the forms of the natural, as their very essence and being."[40] In depth psychological terms, the gods are those natural forms or powers in our life that require our awareness. When we pay attention to those forces, something of our own nature is being heeded. To understand the gods means to see them as those critical moments in life—the deeds, choices, and insights that shape and direct us. In this way, one's inner nature and the nature of the world are connected, bidden by the gods.

Up the stairs, one enters the Archaic Gallery where statues are scattered like heavenly bodies visible to the day. The room is punctuated by blue-gray columns, and the statues rise on white plinths. Of various sizes and postures, mostly of human form but some animal, the archaic figures seem lit from within. A dozen or so sparkling Kore statues are in this room, both small and large. Anyone who has stood before a Kore cannot help but be transfixed by her erect elegance, supple spirit, and ineffable smile. The poet David Jones etched his encounter in these lines:

and the Delectable Kore:
by the radial flutes of her chiton, the lineal, chiseled hair
the contained rhythm of her
is she Elene Argive
or is she transalpine Eleanore

or our Gwenhwyfar
the Selene of Thule
West-Helen?
She's all that and more
all korai, all parthenai made stone.
Agelastos Petra…
and yet you smile from your stone.[41]

In ancient Greece, Kore was not simply a designation denoting an unmarried girl or Virgin goddess. The cultural outpouring shows the Kore to have been a significant figure in religious ritual practices and arts, most prominently in the sculptural tradition of the archaic period, circa 660-480 BCE. The Kore is a standing, draped, young woman in the service of a goddess or god. Kore statues have been found in sanctuaries all across Greece from Athens to Asia Minor,[42] the most distinctive are the Korai from the Athenian Acropolis dedicated to Athena, and those from Hera's temple at Samos. These sculptures were votive offerings to deities that were commissioned by a dedicant. Likened to a contract between a worshipper and a deity, such an offering was related to the practice of *euche,* which was the making of a vow or honoring of a promise.[43] Often the base of the statue would be inscribed with the name of the dedicant, the type of offering that was being made, and to which deity. We know from inscriptions they were commissioned by people from all walks of life: one Kore was once dedicated to Poseidon by a fisherman after a plentiful catch; another by a bread seller to Athena.[44] Kore statues were also created for funerary cult practices as they have been found marking graves.

One of the main questions regarding these statues concerns just who the Kore are—youthful goddesses or idealized images of archaic women? Priestesses? Realistic portraits of young women, such as sisters or daughters of the dedicants, or the dedicants themselves? Scholarly debate circulates on this question of representation, and a dividing line has been carved between idealism and realism. The argument for the ideal emphasizes the nonspecific and generic, thus the figures are considered "embodiments of an aristocratic ideal beauty, anonymous girls meant simply to adorn the sanctuary space and so please Athena,"[45] or whichever divinity they were dedicated to. In contrast, the realism approach focuses on the accumulation of details and the individuality they communicate in relationship to either actual persons or at least in mimesis of life.[46] Art historians also hold differing views as to what features ought to be primary in interpretation and study, such as the coherence of the Korai through the archaic period, or the individuality of each statue. Proponents of realism, such as Mary Stieber, present the view that focuses on the differences which expresses a concern with the imitation of nature, or mimetic realism, rather than type similarity.[47] On the other hand, Gisele Richter, who has been the most influential scholar on the subject, organizes her essential study on the Korai by type over individual forms.[48]

FIGURE 1. PHRASIKLEIA KORE
(MARBLE, ARCHAIC, GREECE, C. 550–540 B.C.)

archaic

Both these approaches bear gifts for an archetypal analysis. The idealist perspective helps to discern the pattern which is revealed by the coherence of the Kore type statue, while the realist emphasis on the individual features of the figures and their particularities become openings for metaphorical exploration and psychological resonance. Yet we are beckoned to listen into what Stieber lyrically refers to as "the poetics of appearance"[49] that belong to the statues distinctive features. The combination of these two approaches is very much in keeping with the depth psychological approach to the study of archetypes which understands that the archetype per se, the typical form or pattern (*arche*), is only discernible through its particular manifestation in life.

Remarkably, Kore statues from across ancient Greece are nearly identical in their essential composition, and their progression in form from static to more naturalistic evolved simultaneously over the 200 years of the archaic period. While the statues differ in size, this continuity of form has become known as the Kore sculptural type. Forerunners of the archaic and classical Kore were around in Crete, Mycenae, and Boeotia dating back to as far as the seventh century BCE, depicted in bronze, terra-cotta, and ivory statuettes, as well as vase paintings.[50]

Originally the Korai were painted in bright colors (*polychromy*), though these have nearly all but faded.[51] Their bodies are wide-shouldered with small high breasts, slender waists and hips, and in the later classical period shapely legs and rounded buttocks. While there is great variety in the clothing the Korai wear, a fine linen tunic (*chiton*) with its crinkly folds is common among all.[52] These folds of their drapery, "parallel, oblique and radiating incisions and ridges,"[53] display infinite variations, both realistic and fantastical in their execution. Considerable varieties of garment fastenings, such as pins and buttons, are also rendered in the stone. Visible from below the hem of their tunics are their feet, a surprising feature that has been noted by many art historians.[54]

Their long hair is arranged in distinctive and elaborate styles, though they all have coiled tresses falling on either side. Some have hair ornaments and wear diadems (*stephane*), and those that were presumably outdoor statues were fitted with metal crowns (*meniskoi*) to keep birds from perching on their heads.[55] Their jewelry would be current to the styles of the period and include necklaces of beads or pendants, spiral or circular bracelets, and pendant or disk-shaped earrings. Some would have been decorated with jewelry affixed by holes in the earlobes or along the brow, but sadly these pieces are mostly missing.

It's not simply the wide array of clothing, hairstyle, and accessories that makes each statue distinct though all are young women. No two Korai look alike; each has an individual face. Their eyes are open, and a sense of pleasure is communicated by their smiles. The distinctiveness of each statue is striking given the uniformity of the statue type.

FIGURE 2. AKROPOLIS KORE
(MARBLE, CLASSICAL, GREECE, C. 535–495 B.C.)

44

FIGURE 3. AKROPOLIS KORE
(MARBLE, CLASSICAL, GREECE, C. 535–495 B.C.)

The postures of these statues are striking, combining as they do a powerful upright stance with a graceful bearing and attentive gaze. There is a limited variety of gestures, some have one arm down along their side, either relaxed or grasping their dress, while the other arm is bent across the chest in a gesture of gratitude or extended with an open palm facing up.[56] Sometimes an object such as a flower, a pomegranate, or a small bird is held in the raised arm as an offering to the deity in whose veneration they were crafted. There are two typical stances of the Kore, either she appears to be standing still or is taking a step forward, one foot slightly ahead of the other.

While these features remain constant in the Korai, each statue is utterly unique and it is this that makes for a striking contrast to the Kouroi, the male standing youths who are their sculptural brothers. Where the Kouroi do have individual faces, they are naked, thus without any of the personal details so prominent with the Korai. Thus while the varying individual features alongside the conservative forms are not exclusive to the Korai sculptural type, they are accentuated to a high degree.

Kore statues exist in a great variety of conditions. Very few are fully intact, most bearing the marks of time and damage. Some statues are whole and nobly bear marred features, while others have been reduced to a fragment of leg beneath radiating linen. No matter how much of them remains, all of the statues are like the elided fragments of Sappho's poetry—their incompleteness, brevity and haunting half presence only heightens their beauty.

Critical features of the Kore archetype can be found in the iconography of these archaic and classical statues. Their distinctive column-like erect bodies, and youthful radiance are analogous to the key themes of individuality, contained integrity, and spirited agency that belong to this archetypal pattern. This study proceeds by exploring the psychological valence of these attributes, so we may perceive how and where the Kore appears in life.

CHAPTER THREE

Grounded Individuality

It is the distinctiveness of each Kore statue that affirms their individuality. Every Kore has a face as individual as any human. Moreover, their dresses, hairstyles, and jewelry all communicate personal style—no two tunics are draped the same, and the colors that they were originally painted would have accentuated the originality of their outfits. While the statue's particularity clearly sets them apart from one another, the psychological significance of their individuality belongs to something deeper than the aesthetics of style. Individuality is based on the knowledge that what makes us different from every other person is some essence of character, which is solely our own. This sense of self is what sets us apart, and because it is rooted in our nature, it is closely aligned with authenticity. The columnar stillness and calm gaze of the Kore expresses something of this connection to one's essential uniqueness. This is not derived from the accoutrements of exterior display, but comes from a sense of interior being. Simply stated, their features make visible the unto-one-selfness that is the essence of the Kore archetype. Psychologically, the physical beauty of the Kore statues communicates the beauty and poise of being oneself.

The particular qualities of individuality that are at work in the Kore can be explored through a number of the sculptural features. To bring this archetypal figure into our awareness so that we are better able to identify her presence in life and claim on us, let's begin gazing downward, to that part closest to the earth, her feet. For the Greeks, feet were a measure of beauty.[57] Sappho calls a bride "of beautiful foot," and Leto, mother of the twins Artemis and Apollo, is praised in the Homeric Hymns for her slender ankles. The valuing of attractive feet naturally leads to their ornamentation, and in Greek literature and art, "light, colorful, and exquisitely crafted sandals [come to] connote swiftness and easy, graceful movement among goddess and mortals."[58] In the older sculptures, Korai wear closed-toe shoes, and trace remains of color reveal at least one surviving statue to have had red shoes. Over time, sandals of various design, with delicate and detailed renderings of feet, became prevalent especially in the statues made during the classical period. That very few Kore are barefoot provides a fascinating detail as to the significance of shoes. The Kore is, in essence, a well-shoed woman. This distinct feature is worth contemplating in some detail, especially as we begin to bridge the iconography into our modern psychology.

FIGURE 4. KORE SHOES
(MARBLE, ARCHAIC, GREECE, C. 570–560 B.C.)

Shoes are recognized as complex signifiers, as postmodernists put it, indicating societal forces and ideas about class, status, gender, and aesthetic sensibility. Footwear can express one's social identity and group alliances, and they can also be an expression of personal identity. In other words, shoes have immense social power. While these postmodern interpretations describe a certain level of fantasy and engagement, they do not get to the deeper root. One's identity is not primarily a sociocultural construction but an inner psychologically felt sense. As one of the most potent symbols for how women feel and walk in the world, shoes are vehicles by which something vital about ourselves is made visible. As shoe historian Linda O'Keeffe puts it, "eyes may be the windows to the soul, but shoes are the gateway to the psyche."[59] That is to say, our soles bare our souls.

Despite their mundane practicality, shoes are totems of identity. They are a tacit means of communicating to others who we are. It is therefore not surprising that for many people shoes symbolize passage into adulthood or a particular vocation or skill. In a series of studies conducted on shoes and identity, Russell Belk reports how people recalled the singular significance of shoes as threshold markers between adolescence and adulthood. This helps our understanding of the conflict that can erupt between adolescents and their parents around shoes. Often what the teen wants, which is effectively an image of who they want to be, is not what the parent deems practical, appropriate or affordable. Beneath the surface friction is an issue of agency, for what the teen needs is to feel the agency of their choice. In this way shoes can act as "separation objects which reflect the newly independent status of the child from the parent."[60] One woman described her initiation into womanhood thus, "I needed to bless my virgin feet with their first pair of high heels."[61] Her shoeing was linked with her emerging korehood.

Many people feel that new shoes promise a new way of being in their life. From this perspective, buying new shoes is a ritual of renewal. That the shoe market is a multi-billion dollar industry in America (92.5 billion U.S. dollars in revenue was projected for 2021)[62] attests to the unconscious participation in this rite by the American collective. One's craft and skill is believed to be rejuvenated by new shoes. Dancers report that new ballet shoes make them feel they will dance better, and athletes overwhelmingly report that new sneakers make them run faster.[63] One ballet dancer said new toe shoes "make me want to be a great dancer."[64] Personifying the call of the spirit, they awaken her sense of possibility in terms of what she can do and who she can be. This example also helps us see how the shoes we wear express our becoming. That is to say, shoes have magical properties that makes them agents of transformation. We only have to look to Cinderella to see how deep in the psyche lives the feeling that shoes can transform your life. As magical objects, shoes can bestow its skillful powers on whoever wears them. Looking back, people often recall how in their youth they felt certain shoes gave them the ability to do things others couldn't, like tap or skate shoes, making them feel they were special, which had a powerful effect on their emerging sense of self. On the other hand, not having the right shoes can be a discomfiting experience that undermines confidence. As one woman declared, "If I do not like the shoes I am wearing and feel ugly or inappropriate it makes me grouchy, unsociable, and insecure."[65]

The admiration women express for other women's shoes likewise reveals the psychological power at work in this magical object. My sense is that it has to do with how the shoe opens the door to desire. We say, "I love your shoes, where did you get them?" all the while imagining how great they would look on ourselves with a particular outfit, how they could be the perfect shoe for an upcoming trip, or even change the whole gestalt of our style. I believe these sudden imaginal flights that strike us on the street or in a restaurant have to do with our desire for renewal and the awakening of possibilities. This aspiration, cloaked in so common an object, is the yearning to concretize our own becoming. The depth of feeling evoked by shoes is indiscernible to the sensate eye, but to the imaginal eye shoes are seen for what they are—symbolic vehicles of our way in the world. If this is the psychological gravity of the shoe, then what are we to make of the staggering fact that 88% of American women buy shoes that are one size too small?[66] How long have women been unconsciously trying to reduce their footprint?

The motif of shoes appears in many myths, legends and fairytales from around the globe. Shoes are so suggestive of a woman's stance in the world that the Immortal Sisters—great spiritual adepts of the Daoist tradition—were known to abandon them in their apotheosis.[67] One story tells of an enlightened noblewoman from an imperial family of the Han Dynasty who revered the Dao but she was married to a man who sought fame and power in the world. When he did not heed her wise counsel to retreat during a fraught political situation, she withdrew to a hermitage in the mountains from where she ascended to the heavens. When her husband eventually traveled to the reclusive estate, all he found were her scarlet slippers. Another Immortal Sister known as the Holy Mother of Dongling attended the sick and needy. She too had a husband who did not honor the Daoist way and who became so upset when she left the house to care for others, he eventually had her jailed. As an alchemist of spirit, she was able to become invisible at will, and shortly after being imprisoned, "she exercised the art of disappearance attributed to a specific class of Taoist adepts and 'flew out the window into the clouds,' leaving only her shoes behind under the window."[68] Transcending their human bonds, these Immortal Sisters left their shoes behinds as remnants of their earthly identities, revealing just how much shoes are about incarnating in life, making oneself felt and known.

Shoe Dreaming

Clarissa Pinkola Estés describes how our feet represent our ability to move freely: "To have shoes to cover the feet is to have the conviction of our beliefs and the wherewithal to act on them. Without psychic shoes a woman is unable to negotiate inner and outer environs that require acuity, sense, caution, and toughness."[69] Given the ubiquitous presence of shoes in our lives and their metaphorical significance, shoes are a common theme in the dreams of women. There is a variety of shoe dream motifs which include the search for the right shoe, finding and wearing the perfect shoe, the inability to find the right shoe, wearing the wrong or ugly shoe, and being shoeless. Each of these dream situations offers insight into the imaginal power of the shoe, its relationship to identity, and points to various moments in the process of inner and outer discernment Estés describes.

In my own dreams, searching for the right shoe has often come during periods where a new attitude to some life situation was needed. To find a new way of walking in the world is analogous to wearing a new pair of shoes. Both the search for the right shoe, and the task of choosing the right shoe, are images of a process of discovery. While at times this may be joyful and full of a sense of possibility, often the search for a new attitude requires an amount of trial and error, which can be challenging. During a prolonged period of major life changes, I had a series of shoe-searching dreams in which, one after another, I simply could not find the right shoes. These dreams were suffused with a deep sense of disappointment as I searched endless racks and display tables, but every shoe was either too small, too large, or not to my taste. These images expressed how at a deeper level my dream-ego felt lost, unsure, and insecure in my changing life situation and how to approach it.

The dissatisfaction that settles somewhat unreasonably in us when we come home empty-handed from a shoe-shopping trip points to some desire having gone unfulfilled. In the same vein, dreams in which women are wearing the wrong shoes are imbued with unease because, having not chosen well, they are not properly shod for the environment— high heels in a sodden field, wooden heeled shoes in a large marble hall clacking loudly, sandals in winter. Not wearing the right shoes suggests having the wrong attitude or being in an inappropriate stance.

In contrast, dreams of finding the perfect shoes, or wearing a great pair of shoes, arrive like blessings. Deeply affirmative in feeling tone, the dreamer is given a sense of confidence in the new ways they are approaching and responding to life. Wearing the right shoe is akin to being in the right mode, protecting one's footing, and allowing for optimal mobility. The right shoe is also the appropriate shoe for the event or terrain, so it connotes readiness.

Finally, there are those numinous dreams wherein one is wearing the perfect, gorgeous, 'dream' shoe. On occasion, these appear to come to the dreamer's conscious attitude as compensations when they've been too critical of themselves. These occurrences have been described as profound encounters wherein the dreamer felt seen by the psyche, affirming something at the core of who they are. Wearing the perfect shoe conveys a sense of connection to what is of enduring value and beauty, and experiences of this kind are often felt to be healing because they remind us of some essential rightness of being.

***

Our connection to the Kore animates our sense of individuality. The power and vitality that characterize the mythic origins of the Kore-Maiden reveal how, psychologically, potency in life depends on how connected we are to the stream of life energy she personifies. Because of this, the Kore is intrinsic to the creation of a strong psychological grounding in young women, thereby making critical the degree to which the values belonging to this archetype are recognized and respected. This is one of the themes the novelist Elena Ferrante explores with penetrating sensitivity in *My Brilliant Friend*, which begins the four-volume story of the complicated friendship of Lila and Lenu in 1950's Sicily.

Lila learns to read when she is three years old by sitting beside her brother while he does his homework, so by the time she starts elementary school it is clear she is exceptionally gifted. While she outshines everyone effortlessly, she plays rough, is always dirty and bruised, and misbehaves in the classroom. Despite being a handful, the teacher endures her behavior because of her talent. Lenu on the other hand works very hard at school and comes second to Lila in everything, and though she is content to follow in Lila's light, she cannot abide being second to anyone else. Where Lila is unruly, violent, sharp, and brilliant, Lenu is polite, modest, self-conscious, and submissive.

As Lila and Lenu approach their middle school years, the course of their lives are irrevocably shaped by a series of events. Lila's father, the neighborhood cobbler, holds to the traditional view that the natural and fitting place for a woman is in the home. Now that his daughter has finished her primary education, those innate gifts that ought be cultivated with further schooling are dismissed as unimportant, and he will not allow her to continue her studies, despite her teacher's interventions.

Daughter needs Father's approval

Defiant, Lila tries to change his mind. In the course of an argument he becomes so enraged that he throws her out of the window. Here is the first decisive wound, for it is not just her arm that her father breaks, but her spirit. The course of Lila's developing identity and psychological ground is shaped by being denied the father's blessing. After this traumatic event, she comes to periodically experience what she calls "dissolving margins," short periods during which the very shapes of people and the world melt away into terrifying formlessness.

This issue of mirroring by the father and being given his blessing is crucial to a young woman's development. Because Lila's daimon, what we may call that spirit of individual beingness, was not mirrored, a split developed between her genius and how she is seen by her family. Under such conditions, a deep sense of self cannot easily flourish. On this issue in a young woman's psyche, Linda Schierse Leonard writes, "If the father is not there for his daughter in a committed and responsible way, encouraging the development of her intellectual, professional, and spiritual side and valuing the uniqueness of her femininity, there results an injury to the daughter's feminine spirit."[70] This wound affects her capacities to move successfully into the world and cope with its conflicts. In his archetypal role as bridge from the inner world of home to the outer world, the father reflects back to his daughter the possibilities that lie for her beyond that threshold. But in stories like Lila's, we see the father as a threshold guardian who bars the way, and the window of possibility deforms into a violent passageway that leads nowhere except to the hospital.

Lila's childhood genius is juxtaposed by Lenu's adolescent effort. Where for Lila the door to education, and by extension the larger world, is shut, for Lenu it is opened by her father's support despite her mother's resistance. Receiving the blessing of the father has profound consequences and lead her to diverge widely from both the world she and Lila grew up in and the ideas that world had about who they can be. As Lenu progresses on to middle school, she labors in her studies and develops a disciplined capacity to work that leads to academic achievement. Part of the enormous effort Lenu must make to succeed in school is due to the absence of Lila whose genius inspired her. Where the flame is not offered, one must grind to find the spark.

Lila tries to find other channels to realize her vision for a different kind of life and begins drawing shoes, which Lenu describes as, "all splendid, all elegant...shoes that once you put them on, she [Lila] said, are so beautiful and so comfortable that at night you go to sleep without taking them off."[71] This description of Lila's drawings reveals how what she is doing is illustrating what it feels like to fully inhabit oneself. Lila's shoes are images of her daimon, her essential calling, and its attempt to be seen in the world.

Intent on devising a prosperous future for her family that struggles in poverty, Lila and her brother Rino begin making a pair of *men's* shoes based on one of her designs which they plan to present to their father. If they can convince him to make shoes based on her unique drawings, they believe their fortunes can change. Lila has unwavering faith in the power of those shoes to transform her family's fate. However, the project is beset with tension because her brother wants to make the shoes quickly and Lila wants them to be perfect, which requires time and effort. Frustrated to the point of fury, on New Year's Eve Rino enters a frenzied state fueled by his hunger for money and social power. Seeing his impatience, his envy, and his desire to dominate on full display, Lila is repulsed and that very night has her first experience of the dissolving margins and she is terrified. The next morning she loses interest in the shoes.

When Rino gives the shoes to their father, Lila is repelled by his vulnerability and how much he needs their father's blessing, which was withheld from her. It's here that we see Lila start to become what Leonard calls the "armored Amazon," a woman who in reaction to the negligent father who has denied her support, provides what she needs for herself: "They build up a strong masculine ego identity through achievement or fighting for a cause or being in control and laying down the law themselves...but this masculine identity is often a protective shell, an armor against the pain of abandonment or rejection by their fathers, an armor against their own softness, weakness, and vulnerability."[72] The result, as we see in Lila, is that these women become estranged from their creativity. The spirited energy that once flowed toward imaginative and innovative play is cut off. The supple Kore who steps into life with a vivacious liveliness turns into the cold and untouchable one.

The problem of the blessing is not something that occurs only in the personal father-daughter relationship. A young woman's developing sense of individuality and significance in the world is also affected by the larger culture in which she lives. Both the personal father and the culture partake in the field of the archetypal Father and facilitate the sense of having an identity and a purpose in the world. This paradigm is at work, Leonard explains, "Wherever there is a patriarchal authoritarian attitude which devalues the feminine by reducing it to a number of roles or qualities which come, not from woman's own experience but from an abstract view of her—there one finds the collective father overpowering the daughter, not allowing her to grow creatively from her own essence."[73]

When the rich and predatory Solara brothers take an interest in that pair of men's shoes she and her brother made, Lila's reaction is violent— she does not want them to see, let alone touch the shoes because she knows they will corrupt whatever they get their hands on. Identified with the shoes, Lila sees them as an extension of herself. They were to be her way of stepping into the world based on her vision and made concrete by her father's craft. Though Lila fights to protect the family dream of a thriving business that provides financial security and a sense of purpose, it is to no avail. Her brother sells her extraordinary designs to the Solara's, and the family loses control of their business. These shoes make visible the forces bound up in Lila's fate, her burgeoning sense of identity and place in the world are unacknowledged by her father and hastily sold by her brother, the consequence of which is that her brilliant gift for innovation goes underground for a long time.

The tragedy of Lila's shoes is like that of the orphan girl in the fairy-tale known as "The Red Shoes." As the story goes, once there was a poor orphan girl who collected scraps of fabric and sewed herself a pair of red shoes which she loved. One day a wealthy old woman offers the orphan girl a home, but it comes at the cost of surrendering her beloved handmade shoes, which eventually leads to the loss of her feet. Handmade shoes are an image of how we make use of our innate talents, learned skills, and the stuff of our day to day experiences to both fashion our life and to live it with authenticity. Lila's shoe designs are expressions of her identity as a creative person who has something to contribute to the world. Where the orphan gives up her shoes for the gilded carriage that comes to whisk her away to a new life, Lila's shoes are given away without her consent. The tragic consequence of the orphan's exchange is mirrored in this chapter of Lila's life. For all her fight to keep the shoes and the autonomy and freedom they promise, Lila cannot prevail at this time over the view held by the male authority figures in her life who see her gifts and her beauty—her personhood—as commodities for sale to the highest bidder.

Of this fateful chapter in their childhood, Lenu writes, "This wealth of adolescence proceeded from a fantastic still childish imagination—the design for extraordinary shoes."[74] The riches of our early years comes at least partly from the sense of selfhood we have that's a bit wild with its potential. Lila's extraordinary shoes symbolize the hope we have of living an extraordinary life directed by the deep callings of our daimon. Our calling, like the perfect pair of shoes, is beautifully wrought, fits us perfectly, expresses our spirit, meets our deep needs, and aids us in traversing the world. For Lila, everything hinged on the story of the shoes.

When the Kore is recognized in young women, their psychic roots are supported and as a consequence they learn to find their footing in themselves and in life. For Lenu, education becomes the opening into a new life. With the blessing of her father and the guidance of teachers who respected Lenu's abilities, the Kore of her being is mirrored. The disciplined rigors of academic work were the precise conditions that allowed her ambitions to develop, through which she comes to discover a deep joy for the new. Despite her self-doubts and insecurities, Lenu lives into her daimon's call. The connection to one's daimon is intrinsic to individuality, because it has to do with being in accord with some part of one's essential nature. Lenu lives into the deeper demands that require her to leave behind the oppression of her childhood neighborhood and family, enabling her to step into a larger world. In so doing she inhabits her life—wears her own handmade shoes as it were—which, though not an emotionally easy one, is hers as a woman, writer, intellectual, feminist, mother, lover, friend, and daughter.

The capacity to respond to the daimon is dependent upon the presence of the Kore, because she stands for independence. We could say that the Kore precedes the daimon, for she symbolizes the foundational sense of one's autonomy. How well we are grounded in our korehood is what fosters attunement to the call of the daimon. In Lenu, we're given a glimpse of how the relationship to these inner forces can be nurtured in a young woman's life, while in Lila we witness a case in which those connections are thwarted. While Lenu and Lila's early years illustrate the problem of the Kore and daimon being recognized in childhood, it would be a mistake to think the emergence of either is wholly reliant on parental mirroring. The warmth of parental encouragement for our independence and spiritedness, as well as the searing anger of rebellion, can both provide the heat for the seeds of korehood to stir to life. Leaving their childhood homes—Lila for a teenage marriage and Lenu for school—the flowering of their korehood and individual genius unfolds in accord to their nature.

Standing One's Ground

In the prevailing Western cultural imagination, men standing their ground is celebrated. This courageous rebellion is exemplified by many great individuals including Socrates, Martin Luther, Dr. Martin Luther King Jr., Vaclav Havel, and Nelson Mandela. Taking a stand, a man stands apart from others and claims his ethos and the values belonging to his worldview. This capacity for individual strength and vision has been seen as necessary to humanity because it valorizes the idea of the human spirit and furthers civilization. In contrast, women standing their ground has historically had a negative connotation, and they have been cast as rebels in opposition to, and resistant of, accepted convention. When *feminist* is used pejoratively to describe women as ideological, selfish, and anti-convention, it is a cloaked term for the disobedient, rebellious woman.

The Kore brings to the cultural imagination an ancient archetypal image of standing one's ground that sees through the negative attitude toward women's expressions of individuality, value, and personal ethos. The feet of the Kore statues are either firmly planted or stepping forward sure-footedly showing us how a woman meets the ground of her self. This is of utmost importance. This sense of self comes through the inner work

KORE

of discerning what we value, what are our ideals, what we want out of life, and acknowledging the gravity of our emotional reality. When one is in touch with the Kore, there is a clarity about what matters.

Marion Woodman understood this as the hallowed territory of the Virgin who she described in the broadest sense as symbolizing the soul and related to the matter of, "Living closely to the reality of who we are born to be. This leads to a strength in living one's truth, and in relationship to the masculine, men in [our] lives, the world, business."[75] *To be*, Woodman reminds us, comes from the Latin word *essa* meaning essence. The Kore provides the deep roots and imaginal background for this grounded essence.

The archetypal insistence to live from the ground of one's being is illustrated in the life of the women's rights activist Malala Yousafazi, the young Pakistani woman who was shot by the Taliban because she stood up for girls' education. Inspired by her father, a teacher and school builder in their home village, Malala loved nothing more than school. He instilled in her the importance of knowledge and the value of ideas. In Islam, both girls and boys have the right to education. However, as the extremist Taliban came to power in Pakistan, they opposed educating girls, bombed their schools, and eventually banned all schools in the region from teaching them. This divergence from Islamic law and basic human rights led Malala and her father to become spokespeople in defense of girls' education. Threatened by the international attention Malala was drawing to the Taliban's rule and its effects on women, they attempted to assassinate her when she was fifteen years old while sitting in a school bus with her classmates. Despite surviving being shot in the head, Malala has not receded into the privacy of her family or nonpolitical life. In spite of tremendous personal risk, she continues to take a stand speaking out as an activist for girls' education around the globe. In recognition of her work, at 17 years of age, she was awarded the Nobel Peace Prize in 2014.

The story of Malala's name carries the mark of her daimon, for she was named after the Afghanistani folk heroine Malalai. It is said that during the late nineteenth-century battle of Maiwand, as the Pashtun Afghans were losing to the British, Malalai picked up their fallen flag and marched onto the battlefield inciting the Pashtun warriors to fight to the death for their freedom so that they would die with pride. Inspired by this young woman's proud spirit, the warriors rose up and defeated the British. Malalai died on the battlefield, sacrificing her life for Pashtun honor. Malala Yousafazi appears to be compelled by that same probity in her social justice work. She said, "My father gave me this name, but I chose this life."[76] She shows how contact with the Kore means having the strength to live one's calling. After the assault on her life, which led her family to seek political asylum in Europe, a Taliban commander wrote to her saying that they would forgive her if she returned to Pakistan, wore a burqa, and went to school for Islamic instruction. She did not reply to the letter, but said that her feeling response after reading the commander's words was, "Who is this man to say that? The Taliban are not our rulers. It's my life, how I live it is my choice."[77] The Kore stands her ground.

At the heart of the Virgin aspect of women's psyches is the capacity to stand in the world rooted in the earth of one's nature. Woodman writes that it is the Virgin who teaches us to live "spontaneously from the emotions and values that are grounded in her own musculature."[78] This connection to our body and feeling is what roots us in the instinctual depths of the psyche, connecting us to our core. Similarly, Marie-Louse von Franz describes the virgin soil of one's nature as "that part of the psyche where there [is] no impact of collective human activities," it is "the place of unconventional inner life,"[79] where we sink into our deep nature so to discover what it is and what it feels like. The virgin forest of our nature is the source of our spontaneity and inner truth.

This brings us to a critical point about beingness. Authoritative dynamics that proceed by exerting power over others via critical judgment—what Woodman calls patriarchal attitudes—silently undermine this fundamental sense of being oneself. The compromising feelings of guilt, shame, and fear that pervade our culture are an outgrowth of this paradigm, which leads to a state wherein we are constantly asking, *who else needs to be pleased*? This means forgetting, or perhaps never discovering, who we are and what it is we want. One of the core ideas Woodman articulates throughout her writing is that being loved instead of being judged leads to a reclaiming of soul. Such love fosters the feeling that, "being ourselves is a reality that is not to be questioned."[80]

To live in Kore awareness is to be true to one's core and in integrity with oneself. In her memoir *I Know Why the Caged Bird Sings*, Maya Angelou describes how her Grandmother Henderson was assailed by a group of young white girls attempting to shame her by exposing their genitals. The culture of racism in the South during the mid-twentieth century left Grandmother Henderson unable to chastise the girls, so as they acted out their ugly abuse, which she had to endure, she began to pray. Watching this incident from inside the house, Angelou recalls, "I found I was praying too, How long could Momma hold out? What new indignity would they think of to subject her to? Would I be able to stay out of it? What would Momma really like me to do?"[81]

Standing still and humming prayers, Grandmother Henderson rested in her religious strength. Throughout the shameful display, she made no response and the white girls eventually moved on. When she came back into the house, Angelou said, "Her face was a brown moon that shone on me. She was beautiful. Something had happened out there, which I couldn't completely understand, but I could see that she was happy."[82] Grandmother Henderson prevailed. Like the Kore statues, she stood tall and still, contained within her undiminished dignity as a person. Angelou's portrait of her Grandmother draws out a particular kind of Kore groundedness. It is the integrity of living from the ground of one's being, which comes to act as a psychological center, flexible and strong enough to move through the world in spite of what it throws at us. This consolidated sense of self gives rise to a quality of presence that is both graceful and intense, just like the full moon.

Kore Multivalence

In the early chthonic and Titan strata of Greek myth and religion, it was the Great Mother goddess who held dominion. The birth of the Olympian gods heralded a shift from worship of the Great Mother to that of the Kore, made evident by the preeminent place Athena, Artemis and Hestia occupied in the new pantheon.[83] Among these most revered Kore goddesses in this new pantheon was Persephone. While Persephone stands alongside these other goddesses who personify the individuality and vitality that are the quintessence of the archetype, there is something about her in particular that makes korehood seem not a remote ideal but an intrinsic aspect of soulmaking. I believe it is because Persephone's myth is a poetic analogy for the movement of the psyche towards korehood, she lays claim to a singular mysterious power in the imagination. Of all the Kore figures of myth, it is to Persephone women return.

A major figure in the religious traditions of ancient Greece for nearly 2,000 years, Persephone and her mother Demeter were venerated in the Eleusinian Mysteries, a religious cult housed in the Sanctuary of Eleusis near Athens. This cult's ritual practices are closely associated with the myth as told in the *Homeric Hymn to Demeter*, dated to the eighth century BCE, which tells the tale of Demeter's search for Persephone after she is abducted by Hades and taken to the underworld. While mother and daughter are eventually reunited, Persephone cannot return and stay with Demeter as before because, when she was with Hades, she ate the fateful pomegranate seeds which bound her to him and his realm. Thus, throughout the year Persephone moves between worlds, eternally descending below to her husband and rising above to her mother. Polymorphic Persephone is daughter, wife, queen of the underworld, and Kore.

The Homeric Hymn recounts how Demeter establishes the Eleusinian Mystery cult when Persephone first returns from Hades in order to give humankind the same succor and faith she herself experienced. Connecting Persephone's underworld passage with the cycle of life, death and rebirth, the rituals appear to have provided an initiation that gave its participants a religious experience of the ongoing force of life. About the Eleusinian rituals, Sophocles is claimed to have said, "Thrice happy are those mortals who having seen these rites depart for Hades; for to them alone is it granted to have true life there."[84] What were these rites exactly and how did they express a faith in life despite death remains a mystery because initiates were prohibited from sharing what transpired in the rituals, including the apotheosis that is believed to have been the rites' central feature. This secrecy is made plain in the description the travelogue writer Pausanias made of his visit to the Eleusinian sanctuary in the 2nd

My painting

century AD, "My dream forbids the description of the things within the wall of the sanctuary, and the uninitiated are of course not permitted to learn that which they are prevented from seeing."[85] Pausanias's lip are sealed by both the dream message and religious tradition. However, we have an inkling that in the course of the initiation ceremonies there was a rebirth symbolized in one of the final rituals by an ear of grain, which was understood to be Persephone rising from the underworld. Kerényi says this vision would have worked to free the initiates of their fear of death because they were shown there can be a birth in death, "and it was possible also for human beings if they had faith in the Goddesses."[86]

The work of a poet is to render visible the essential nature of things. Until the ancient Greek poets put the name Persephone into their poems, she was simply called *arrhetos koura*, the ineffable maiden. Euripides called her "the unspeakable girl."[87] Persephone is ineffable as the inward facing goddess who traverses the underworld, and this secret aspect is central to her revelation in the Eleusinian Mysteries. Like the grain that emerges out of the dark earth into the light, she rises up from Hades. Where Persephone is turned toward the inner recesses of the earth, Demeter is turned towards the sunlit fields and high growing grain. Together these two goddesses face, as it were, the two planes of existence.

While the Mother-Daughter relationship is one of the principal themes in this myth, which I discuss in part III, the potency of this archetypal configuration has had an effect on our imagination that very often goes unnoticed. What sets Persephone apart from other goddesses who draw from the larger archetypal pattern of the Kore is her polymorphism. Where Athena and Artemis are unchanged in their identities, Persephone continually changes and inhabits multiple conditions simultaneously—she is herself, daughter, wife, and queen. Yet, despite her complexity, there is a tendency in mythological and depth psychological scholarship, reflected by Demeter herself, to narrowly regard Persephone primarily as simply daughter or as her younger self. This fascinating example of the Mother-Daughter pair makes visible the inherent challenges of recognizing korehood. These important matters regarding the Mother and the Kore, and the distinction of the Kore and Daughter are likewise treated in greater depth in part III. At this point let me simply state that Kore

Kore and Daughter are not synonymous, they are distinct archetypal modes of being. However, the Kore is regularly absorbed by the Daughter. This reduction, which is a given when one is seeing with the Mother-eye, obscures Persephone's plurality given by the Kore archetype, and confines her to a role that, while important, is only *one* part of her character.

There is no goddess in Greek myth who more clearly shines a light on the paradoxical combination of being one-in-herself and a plurality than Persephone. This goddess renders with striking clarity the Kore's multivalence, which has to be seen in relation to her individuality. The Kore stands apart, and Persephone's polymorphic quality *comes from her ability to stand in herself*. This is what allows her to inhabit the different roles in her world. Sticking to the image that the myth presents, we are emboldened to look at Persephone with new eyes so to perceive the older sovereign source of her innate multiplicity. Something else opens up when we seek the roots of the psychic condition of Kore multivalence in its mythic ground.

We find in the ancient sources that there was a fluidity with which Persephone's name was communicated.[88] Kore, Daughter and Persephone were often used interchangeably, which makes for an assumed synonymity. We have already seen the protean quality of the term *kore* in its multiple meanings of girl, maiden, and virgin, and its interchangeability with *parthenia*, highlighting the multivalence that belongs to this pattern of consciousness. That the archaic and Homeric Greek tradition emphasized referring to Persephone as Kore suggests two things. The first is the ancient primacy of Persephone's Kore nature which unfolds through the course of her myth. The second is that her korehood is distinct from, and yet encompasses, her identities as daughter, wife and queen. Farnell shows how both of these are accorded in the pre-Greek cult of Persephone, who was originally an ancient underworld goddess with distinct origins independent of Demeter.[89] While the Mother-Daughter pair was always at the center of Demeter's cult and myth, it was only in the late archaic period that the goddess Persephone became linked to it. Downing suggests that the synthesis of the Demeter cult with that of Persephone had something to do with "a felt connection between Kore and Persephone perhaps based on the idea that a death goddess will also be a source of fruitfulness."[90]

64

This blending gave rise to the myth and ritual tradition we have inherited wherein Persephone-Kore is Demeter's daughter.

Because Persephone goes from being a daughter to a bride and queen, Kerényi proposes that the mother and husband are the two relationships which define Persephone's identity.[91] Kerényi contrasts her with Athena, who he argues, is absolutely free from sexual attachment or desire for a masculine partner. There is a second kind of freedom that marks Athena's korehood, for being born out of her father's head she is strangely free of the bonds of the mother. Kerényi sees Persephone as embodying both the mother and husband relationships in extreme, and as if along a borderline she balances both—the maiden as daughter becomes bride as wife. While these are certainly important aspects of Persephone's character, defining her solely in terms of her relationships also limits and even contradicts the archetypal core of the Kore-Virgin. Once again we encounter a subsuming of Persephone's Kore essence by a privileging of the Daughter and Wife aspects.

The tendency to see the Kore as formed by relationship rather than by standing apart is related to descriptions of her being in an eternal process of becoming. Often interpreted as symbolizing continuing possibility, the Maiden stands with one foot on either side of the threshold between child and woman. For Betty Smith, this is the Kore's most distinctive aspect, "From young girlhood she has moved into a blossoming that belongs to the maiden and will soon be claimed as bride, for the bride is the crossing of the threshold."[92] Viewed this way, korehood becomes a transitional phase; the Kore is always on her way to being something else. This developmental perspective is also depicted in the personified lunar cycle, the new moon Maiden becoming the full moon Mother, who eventually becomes the waning moon Crone. As a child she is dependent on her mother and father, and as lover, wife, and mother her identity is realized in the beloved, husband, and child. This developmental metamorphosis certainly reflects women's lived experiences and how we understand changing biological and relational phases. However, the inner figures we find in myth do not always mirror the outer roles of life, and this developmental and relational emphasis risks obscuring the most critical feature of the Kore, which is an integrity that transcends phases of life.

This way of seeing emphasizes korehood as an essential and fully articulated quality of the psyche. The Kore is neither a needy child nor a dependent wife. Unto-oneself is not a phase that belongs to one narrow period, but a quality of consciousness that is accessible all throughout life. As a vital force, the Kore is the vitality of the budding flower who unfolds into itself. She personifies not becoming but being. It is this pattern in the psyche that connects us to that essential sense of self distinct from who we know ourselves to be through our relationships to others.

Persephone's korehood is rendered visible by the changes in her identity and relational configurations so long as we see through our own tendency to impose socialized and personalistic tropes on the deeper image. Rather than being defined by others, Persephone is polymorphic, inhabiting the roles of daughter and wife within the wider essence of her korehood. It's in these shoes that she traverses the underworld, the windswept and sun-baked fields, and the Olympian palaces, for she is the triple *arrhetos koura*—daughter of Demeter, wife of Hades and goddess in her own right, "holy Persephone," queen of the underworld. That her year is divided into thirds confirms her threefold nature.[93] The Homeric Hymn says that a third of her year she was to stay in the misty darkness of the underworld with Hades, and two-thirds with her mother and other gods. Her ascent (*anodos*) marks the period where she is reunited with Demeter who rejoices by bringing forth the blossoms of spring, and her descent (*kathodos*) is when she joins Hades. While her year is divided along these planes, the third aspect of her nature, holy Persephone, is the essential constant. The ineffable mystery of this goddess is that she is one-in-herself.

CHAPTER FOUR

Contained Integrity

The quiet calm that radiates from the Kore statues reveals another quality intrinsic to the archetype—integrity. Whether standing still or stepping forward, bearing sinuous gestures or rigid articulation, clothed simply or in complicated drapes, the Kore's stillness, perceptiveness, and tranquility communicate her depth and essential wholeness. This is particularly evident in how the figures simultaneously reveal and conceal themselves. On the one hand, their form imparts an immutable sense of identity through their erect postures and strong lines. At the same time, they generate a mysterious atmosphere by means of the secrets in their smiles, the hidden folds of their garments. Questions abound—where are they headed and to which divinity are they are making their offerings? Their serene gazes are full of some knowing, and the curve of their lips are full with a self-satisfaction that seems to say that the silent rhythm of the Kore takes its form from an ineffable source. As if expressing a secret joy, the statues convey the power of interiority.

The simple elegance of the Cheramyes Kore conveys this interior potency. In a gesture of devotion, her left hand holds a bird to her chest. The lines of her chiton drape over her slender form, pouring to the ground in an even cascading rhythm. Her right hand rests at her side, every line of her tunic and body are steadfastly connected. Her fingers are tightly pressed to one another, and there isn't a single extra fold. She is sheathed in her essence.

FIGURE 5. CHERAMYES KORE
(MARBLE, ARCHAIC, GREECE, C. 575–555 B.C.)

This sense of integrity and undivided wholeness could be described as what it means to know oneself. When we know our own mind, what is at work is an inner coherence born from self awareness. Authenticity that stems from inner understanding has a different image at its heart compared to what is lauded in mainstream culture. A survey of self-help and popular psychology literature reveals there are many fantasies that harbor the Delphic call to "know thyself," and at the top reigns balance, the peak goal of the self-development journey. In contrast to the state of leveled perfection that balance implies, integrity means neither symmetry, completion nor equilibrium. Rather, it means everything belongs. This wider sense of self-understanding is usually earned with experience and age, but can be equally known in the spirit of youth.

A woman who was unwed was imagined to be undivided from herself, her korehood whole and holy. This is reflected in the Greek meanings of *kore* and *parthenos* which included, writes classicist Guilia Sissa, "a treasure that one guards (*phylassein*), a value that must be respected (*terein*)."[94] This complex ancient understanding, as divinized in the Virgin goddesses of the ancient Mediterranean world, reveals one-in-herselfness as central to the archetypal stream of the Kore. For the Kore, inner nature is guide. Nor Hall hones in on this quality and its metaphorical meaning, "To be virginal does not mean to be chaste, but rather to be true to nature and instinct."[95] In other words, korehood means authenticity, that how I feel, what I say and what I do are aligned. When I am with another, I am equally present to myself as I am to that other.

Cultivating this quality of integrity rooted in our essential nature requires processes of containment where resonances of being, feeling and doing can develop. One form of this is privacy, wherein such recognitions can be made through inner dialogue. Kore containment is the way in which we turn inward to sort out feelings and evaluate what is of importance, asking *What matters here? Where do I want to devote my energy, my time?* In working with the psyche we are, "guided by the response of the unconscious as revealed in dreams, we differentiate grain from grain, question after question, until one day we find our authentic voice," Marion Woodman counsels. [96] This capacity to draw in and connect to one's nature is what she refers to as "the virgin's meditative strength"[97] which is what allows a woman to be in contact with the psyche and its archetypal energies without becoming inflated and losing herself. Our Kore nature is what ensures our psychological integrity remains intact.

In the midst of a fragmentary world where we are inundated with persona images and collectivized values, the mediative strength of the Kore is what keeps us from falling under those divisive influences. Without a grounding in her vessel, we fall too easily under the spirit of the times and its pressured overexposure, whether psychological, emotional, or physical. "Some vital energy is drained from us when we disconnect from moon-like rhythms of invisibility…we get damaged by too much daylight," writes mythteller Martin Shaw.[98] This well applies here.

Containment is the necessary condition for the slow gestation of being that occurs in the deep recesses of one's virginal interiority. This indwelling is the precondition for action rooted in authenticity. While paradoxical, this ability to act in accord with one's nature is cultivated by stillness. This indwelling calm is what Jungian analyst Robert Johnson identifies as one of the primary ways feminine consciousness connects to its truth: "The feminine principle seems to have to go back to a very still inner center every time something happens to her; and this is a creative act. She must go back to it, but must not drown in it. She is receptive, not passive."[99] The 'she' Johnson is referring to is the mythic figure Psyche, who seeks reunion with her beloved Eros through a series of impossible trials ordained by Aphrodite. Psyche is confronted with certain failure at each of the four tasks, and in those moments where she is utterly alone and without outer direction, animals and plants come to her aid. This shows how returning to a receptive stillness allows for insight, which emerges through the sacrifice of one's will to action and instead pays attention and listens. This motif shows how the deep intelligences of nature come to our support when we turn to them. It also suggests that stilling ourselves in order to listen into the unconscious is itself a creative act.

The virgin goddess Hestia also shows us the twining of stillness and interiority. The etymology of her name reveals the tight constellation of these themes, which classicist L.R. Farnell traced to *vas*, which means 'to inhabit'.[100] The Greek root of Hestia's name, *estia*, is defined as "a hearth, a household or family, an altar, places which are to a country as hearth is to a home; for Pythagoreans it means the central fire of the universe, the heart in the body."[101] These reveal that in the Greek imagination, Hestia personified a sacred interiority made visible by the hearth flame of home and temple, her power felt as the radiating warmth at the center of life. The contained fires of her hearth-cult, whether belonging to the intimate family or the public, symbolized the center around which people congregated. Her sacred fires extended beyond the local milieu and marked the center of the world, which for the Greeks was Delphi and the sacred temple precinct of Apollo. There at the *omphalos* or navel stone, Hestia was presented as a heap of glowing charcoal that represented the fire that burned at the center of the earth.[102]

There is an interesting tension between the sacred interiority of this Kore goddess and her place in the public and private spheres. In Hestia, the sanctity of what is private is kept before the mind's eye, a theme insightfully discussed by Jungian scholar Stephanie Demetrakopolous:

> In a curious passage that emphasizes Hestia's purity, Hesiod says in *Works and Days* that a man should avoid showing his genitals to Hestia if they are besprinkled (sometimes translated 'befouled') with semen...Some of Hannah Arendt's ideas about the difference between the private and the public spheres in *The Human Condition* shed light on the virginity motif. Arendt equates the private realm with shame of the body: 'It is striking that from the beginning of history to our own time it has always been the bodily part of human existence that needed to be hidden in privacy, all things connected with the necessity of the life process itself.' Farnell's idea that Hestia comes from '*vas*,' to inhabit, ties in with this theme. Hestia is the inviolable private source, the solemn center in which exists the ultimate mystery of being human. Each person returns daily to this home base for the soul's rejuvenation, a rejuvenation archetypally associated with 'virginity.'[103]

Hestia's birth story further highlights her power of indwelling. First-born of Kronos and Rhea, she was the first to be ingested by her father, meaning she spent the longest time *inside*. After she and her Olympian siblings were liberated from imprisonment in their father's belly by their brother Zeus, they took their rightful places in the cosmological order of the world. Plato said all the Olympian gods could fly around but, "Hestia alone abides at home."[104] As the indwelling force of the gods, she is, in Demetrakopolous' words, "the center that sustains the place of return."[105] In other words, Hestia's power is an in-drawing one, she gathers.

We can imagine that when we withdraw from the busy worldly pressures of our daily life in order to touch back into our interiority, we are inviting Hestia into our consciousness. "Within you," says Siddhartha, "there is a stillness and sanctuary to which you can retreat at anytime and be yourself."[106] Personifying the power that draws us *in*, Hillman argues, it is Hestia who carries the archetypal insistence towards preserving the sanctity of interiority. Hearth, he reminds us, "in Latin is *focus*, which can be translated into psychological language as the centering attention that warms to life all that comes within its radius—this is Hestia."[107] Her necessity in psychological life is this ability to mediate an indwelling of attention, which is at work in a variety of practices including journaling, dreamwork, meditation, and astrological contemplation, which all invoke the quiet warmth of Hestian attention. We step into these imaginal spaces to hush ourselves in order to attend the inner fire—or just sit by this fire. Let's imagine stillness then as a quality of the relationship we have with the Kore-Virgin.

✳✳✳

Many of the archaic Kore statues stand with one hand grasping their dress, as though peeling the fabric away from their body. While this gesture is practical in order to step forward, the metaphorical rhythm of the image suggests something else may be at work. Just as we peel away outer layers to get to the insides of things, the Kore indicates there is something beneath her outer layer, an inside beneath the surface. She is drawing attention to a world hidden from view, and, while her gesture intimates a concealed depth, she is not revealing that which is hidden.

Her quiet gesture simply indicates that there exists an inner aspect that remains inviolable.

The god's appearances, their physicality and gestures, convey the archetypal qualities they personify. Hermes is his quickness, Hades his invisibility, Aphrodite her beauty. The Kore displays her sheathed interiority. Demetrakopolous offers another description of Hestia that contributes to this aspect of the Kore, "part of her mystery is her hiddenness; the reflective, brooding insights born into her consciousness are in essence a private ethos that remain unshared."[108] The Kore personifies that force which urges us to keep some part of ourselves hidden from view and inaccessible to others.

Overt contrasts help to clarify more essential distinctions, and in this vein the special configuration of Aphrodite and the Kore invites a closer look. Unlike Aphrodite whose resplendent sex *is* the erotic imagination, the Kore remains clothed in a protective sheath. This fundamental polarity of the Aphroditic realm and korehood was rendered sharply in Greek myth. In the opening lines of the *Homeric Hymn to Aphrodite* the poet tells how while this goddess holds sway over all living beings—animals, mortals and gods—she has no power over the three Kore goddesses Artemis, Athena and Hestia. In other words, the world of the Kore and the world of Aphrodite do not meet. The erotic fusion of Aphrodite consciousness collides with the impenetrable self containment of the Virgin.

Could we go so far as to say that where Aphrodite reigns, the Kore is by necessity excluded? The border between these two archetypal territories is clearly demarcated. However, just as travel between countries can be encouraged or obstructed depending on diplomatic agreements, so contact and border crossings between these two fields can be negotiated. The key appears to lie in recognizing the value of each field of life, which in turn cultivates the other. This is the possibility Ginette Paris sees in the midst of the particular confusion people encounter around whether what they want is deeper intimacy or time alone:

> This apparent confusion may be explained by the bond between these: true contact implies also moments of complete solitude, and vice versa, to really taste solitude, one must

be at peace with those important to us and leave them with a light heart. The woman who seems to be most confused is often the one who is both denied a profound contact with husband and friends and deprived of solitude and time for herself...[109]

If the function of Aphrodite is to connect us with others, and the Kore is to connect us with ourselves, both goddesses need due attention. While the territories of Aphrodite and the Kore cannot overlap, their borders can be mediated so as to recognize they are friendly countries who depend on one another, and who invite frequent passage for mutual benefit.

***

Contained integrity is likewise a quality rendered in powerful lines by Athena, whose birth story is among the most memorable in all Greek myth. When Zeus learns that the child born of his lover Metis will be greater than him, he decides the best course of action to avoid this outcome is to swallow the pregnant goddess. Thus when Athena is born, it is from her father's head. Furthermore, she emerges fully armored. The Homeric poet recounts how all the natural world was in awe of her arrival, "Great Olympos itself shook terribly under the might of bright-eyes, the earth groaned awfully and the ocean was moved to foam up with dark waves, then as sudden the salt sea stopped. The glorious son of Hyperion, the sun, stood his fast-footed horses still for a long time, until the girl took that god-like armor from her immortal shoulders. Shrewd Zeus laughed."[110] Athena's armor and her korehood are both her birthright. In fact, one is the concrete expression of the other, for her armor is a kind of carapace shell that shouts her virginal impenetrability.

There is another of Athena's features that has resonances to the kind of integrity that belongs to the Kore archetype. Athena was called bright-eyes, *Glaukopis*, which refers to her ability to clearly see the possibilities inherent in any situation. The owl naturally becomes her tutelary animal as its large eyes expresses a high degree of intelligence, and ensures its hunting prowess. Shrewdly calculating correct action, Athena is the perceptiveness which strategic thinking requires. This marked clarity engenders effective response rather than rash reaction to the changing conditions in life. As mentor to many of the warrior heroes, Athena's voice counsels reason and restraint, which paired with a cool guiding hand assures that the principles of civilization rise over passion. This can be seen in the principles of the democratic justice system and its valuing of the ideals of impartiality and reason symbolized by Blind Justice (Metis and Athena are combined in this figure) who holds the scales, a tool of objective and balanced measurement. Athena is one of the goddesses untouched by Aphrodite's ardent desires. Clarity, shrewd perception, measured steps, and patience are all characteristic of Athena's triumph, which classicist Walter Otto describes as "perfection in the living present."[111] Athena shows how in her field of consciousness, right perception or being in integrity with the moment, means contained, even controlled, stillness.

***

The interior potency of the Kore is a renewable resource. This is what third wave feminist philosopher Luce Irigaray describes as woman's perpetual flowering, "a woman grows, blossoms, and fertilizes (herself) within her own body...she cannot be reduced to a single flower, as in the male image of virginity. In line with her own virginity, she is never completed in a single form. She is ceaselessly becoming, she 'flowers' again and again, if she stays close to herself and the living world."[112]

The myths show this is so. Even golden Aphrodite, our most erotic Greek goddess, renews her virginity each year by retreating to sacred springs. Hera, the archetypal wife who sanctifies marriage, also withdraws from her husband Zeus to a hallowed place whose pools are where she becomes virginal again. These images remind us how the archetype in its mythic embodiment is distinct from human expression, goddesses fluidly inhabit roles that are either contradictory or impossible for a woman who is naturally constrained by biological and sociocultural realities. Aphrodite and Hera, two goddesses for whom erotic entanglements, seduction, and marriage are primary to their nature, are also Kore from time to time. These two likewise exemplify how the gods carry their own contradictions in perfect equilibrium, what Kerényi called a borderline situation where one aspect of a god rests in perfect poise to its opposite aspect.[113]

The mythic pools to which Aphrodite and Hera retreat belong to the imaginal space where woman as lover, wife, mother returns to korehood and becomes, "closed, possessed and lightened, receptive, virginal."[114] These sacred pools into which the goddesses submerse themselves effect a metamorphosis by means of the purifying powers of water. That these goddesses withdraw from their lovers and husbands shows how separation from others is necessary for a return to oneself. Within this lies a paradoxical truth, that coming back to oneself is what allows us to move more fully toward others. To have a fruitful relationship to either of these goddesses, one has to be open to this kind of renewal.

Portraits of Sovereignty

As a soul figure grounded in its sense of integrity, the Kore knows what belongs to her, what she needs, what her aims are. Her self containment produces both an inner clarity and firmness which disallows introjections of the shoulds and oughts pronounced by outside authorities. For women, this can appear in the refusal to accept the traditional roles relegated them by the patriarchal worldview. For men, the Kore's firmness can be imagined as living in that deep personal sense of what belongs to one's soul and what doesn't. Once you know what belongs to you, you can go after it regardless of collectivized expectations. I believe that one of the functions of the Kore is to preserve our capacity to resist the pressures of the spirit of the time. To discern Kore sovereignty, let us look at the lives of some extraordinary women in both their genuine steadfastness of vision and in the rendering of their legend.

Eleanor of Aquitaine (1122/1124-1204) was a unique woman for the twelfth century. Born in Poitiers, France, she was the heiress of vast land-holdings, and her political influence and power were exercised throughout her life as wife of two kings and mother of three kings. The chronicler Richard of Devizes, a contemporary of the Queen, described her as "an incomparable woman, beautiful yet virtuous, powerful yet gentle, humble yet keen-witted, qualities which are most rarely found in a woman."[115] Throughout Western history, women's lives were generally not considered of enough importance to chronicle, thus written records provide little detail of Eleanor's personality and life. Nonetheless, we can surmise that her maverick character was partially due to the world she was raised in. Eleanor's grandfather was Duke William IX, the first lyric troubadour of Provence and founder of the troubadour tradition often called *fine amour*, or noble love.[116] In troubadour culture, a woman was not seen as an object but as a partner "able to make decisions, an honorable person whom the true lover must 'court' patiently before he could deserve her favors," writes historian Jean Flori.[117] Eleanor grew up in this subculture where women were valued, extolled for their innate virtues, and seen as equal to men. In this legendary time and place of literary creativity, new sensibilities about love and spirituality as embodied by women were being explored. Noble love and the imperious longings of the heart were praised over marriage as dutiful religious transaction, and women were seen not as objects for possession or merely the subjects of poetry, but poets and patrons themselves. These were radical ideas given the time. This brilliant counterculture also gave birth to the legendary court of love, a tribunal said to have been presided over by Eleanor and her daughter Marie of Champagne, which ruled over cases of the heart where lovers could bring their grievances for justice.

While this gem of troubadour culture was the milieu within which Eleanor was raised, it was nonetheless housed within a broader patriarchal and religiously dogmatic one ruled by the Catholic Church. Described by Flori as "sensual and innovatory,"[118] Eleanor was a woman of character and displayed none of the docility that was expected of women in the wider society at the time. Her vibrancy and autonomy, combined with her renowned physical beauty, made her an object of critique, since all

EVE

of these were deemed unfavorable traits in women. In this period of the Western Christian world, women were called daughters of Eve and their beauty regarded as temptations to sin. It was Eve who transgressed God's command in the Garden of Eden, and thereby condemned humanity to backbreaking labor and suffering outside of Paradise. By association, all women were the source of sin and responsible for repenting for this original sin through submission to male authority (fathers, husbands, brothers) and the Church. Any woman who did not comport herself in a passive manner was judged harshly, as historical records show. Flori writes, "chroniclers regarded the lively Eleanor with deep prejudice strengthened by the somewhat heretical aura lent her by the notion ... of her possible literary influence as a 'queen of courtly love.'"[119]

Given the Provençal culture and its contrasting views of women, when her father William X died, Eleanor was made Duchess of the hereditary lands of Aquitaine and Poitiers in her own name. This meant that no matter the circumstances, including marriage, her lands and her wealth remained her own throughout her life.[120] As the most desirable and eligible Duchess, shortly after her father's death, she either 15 or 17 years of age, she was married to the heir of the French throne, Louis VII in 1137, and was crowned queen. Nine years later, Eleanor joined Louis on the second crusade to Jerusalem in 1146, and some accounts say that she and her ladies-in-waiting dressed as Amazons, those magnificent warrior women of Greek myth renowned to be equal, if not superior, to any male fighter. [121]

As I noted above, women were expected to defer in obedience to their husbands, both privately and publicly. Even a woman who was a monarch was expected to be ruled by her husband who was her spiritual and temporal lord, and to defer all matters of state to him and her male advisors. Eleanor clearly did not subscribe to this view. In 1152 she divorced Louis VII to marry Henry Anjou, who shortly thereafter became Henry II, King of England, making her Queen again. One can imagine the talk both high and low that abounded throughout Christendom. Regardless, it appears Eleanor had the sense of ultimate authority of her own life, and her divorce shows her determination to live accordingly. It is in this regard that we can understand Jungian scholar Ann Ulanov's extension of Harding's psychological amplification of the Virgin, describing this archetype as constellating in the personality of a woman as, "an independence based on fidelity to the feminine principle, one which yields an identity where the woman feels she is a person in her own right and not simply a counterpart to the male. Her sovereign allegiance is to something feminine—the expression and fulfillment of her own feminine goals and purposes rather than the fulfillment of a male person."[122] The woman who has learned to receive the Kore is psychologically sovereign. From the French *soverain,* this means highest, supreme, chief, and when used in speaking of remedies and medicines, it means *potent in a high degree.* To be sovereign is to know and regard one's own truth. As we will soon see, Eleanor did not compromise personally or politically. Her wealth alone could not have given her the temerity or inclination to live as she did. This spiritedness that flew in the face of convention came from within.

It is clear that Eleanor's Kore potency was unpopular. Flori discusses how her "quasi-libertarian behavior"[123] was so counter to that of the clerics and their moral strictures and ideology that they gleefully cast her as a woman who, driven by base sexual desires, was uncontrollable by her husband. The "black legends" of Eleanor were formed around this fantasy of sexual voraciousness. One salacious tale claims that during the crusade to Jerusalem, she had an affair with the emperor Saladin (who was a child at the time), as well as with her uncle Raymond. She is also said to have tortured and eventually murdered Henry's longtime mistress Rosamund Clifford. There is no proof for any of these tales, though these thinly veiled defamations of her character have survived through the ages.

As wife to Henry II and Queen of England, Eleanor would act as Regent whenever Henry was away in battle, which appears to have been quite frequent. She traveled often between England and Aquitaine, embarking on extensive tours of her kingdom and acted as royal administrator most of her life. Her success as a monarch and political force was partly due to her shrewd understanding of the importance of relationships. The various rulers of the twelfth-century world most often stood alone with hired mercenaries trying to take what they wanted from others and defend what was theirs. Feigning relationship and loyalty, Henry II and Louis VII spent twenty years back and forth as friends and enemies, going from truce to war to renewed truce. Eleanor knew that she could not afford such bravado. In contrast to that form of kingly politics, Eleanor cultivated and maintained relationships with everyone—her counselors, vassals, her children, the Pope, and even her first husband Louis.[124]

Every account of Eleanor's life portrays how it was one entirely devoted to politics and shaped by stratagem and intrigue. At various times, Eleanor schemed with her sons for the English throne against Henry, her husband and their father. While all of those attempts were unsuccessful, her influence was so strong that Henry had her imprisoned in 1173. Forced to withdraw from both public and private life, she was put under house arrest and lived alone but for one companion for sixteen years. One surmises that Eleanor's spiritual life was a significant anchor through this period and its untold challenges. During her enforced incubation, Eleanor quite literally lived the indwelling stillness of Hestia. In striking contrast to her life at court, this time was like an initiation into the contained potency of the Kore. Despite this long period of isolation and quiet, Eleanor would emerge with vibrant and unconquered spirits upon Henry's death in 1189. Called her "period of triumph,"[125] in the final fifteen years of her life she was a crone Queen, husbandless and sovereign ruler of the lands of England and Aquitaine in her son King Richard's frequent battle-making absences. Eleanor lived into her ninth decade, a very long life for any era, and throughout it she appears to have had a dignity of spirit that prevailed even when she had nearly all her freedoms taken away.

These qualities of the Kore are not always as fully realized or consciously embraced as they appear to have been for Eleanor of Aquitaine. Very often it is through violation or disregard that one comes into relationship with the field of energy this archetype symbolizes. The search for one's sovereignty and authenticity is then born from either its initial absence, or comes from having had it denied or misshapen by life circumstances. That our relationship with the Kore is very often fostered by our having been disconnected from our authenticity, sense of sovereignty, creative potential, or spiritedness is an important part of how she becomes a reality in our psyche.

The life of Lucrezia Borgia (1480-1519) is a portrait of how one's connection to the Kore is forged out of living in conditions where it has been denied. Born in the springtime outside of Rome, Lucrezia was the daughter of Vannozza Cattanei and Rodrigo Borgia, better known as Pope Alexander VI.[126] Lucrezia's life was inextricably linked to her father's dynastic plans and shifting political alliances, and she was used as a pawn in his strategies for most of her early years until she learned to play the game on her own terms. Popular legend paints Lucrezia as a murdering seductress with a penchant for poison, and some say she took both her brother Cesare and her father to her bed. While these stories are what secured Lucrezia's infamy, they are black legends with the same scent as Eleanor's, promulgated by Christian clerics.

Lucrezia was married three times. The first marriage agreement was drawn up when she was eleven years old, and in 1493 she married her first husband, Giovanni Sforza, when she was thirteen.[127] He left her four years later, purportedly because there was a plan by her father to have him killed.[128] This is likely not too far from the truth, as once the alliance with the Sforza family no longer served the Pope's political appetites, he needed his daughter to be free for a new marriage. This first marriage was annulled in 1497, and a year later Lucrezia married the Duke of Bisceglie.[129] In August of 1500, he was murdered by her brother's men, and though her brother Cesare claimed her husband had tried to kill him, Lucrezia was devastated and she withdrew from her family in Rome to her castle at Nepi.[130]

Historian Sarah Bradford paints a compelling picture of the handful of months Lucrezia was in retreat from life in the Papal palace. Cloistered from the political theatre, Bradford describes how Lucrezia came to understand her husband's murder as a "deliberate act of terror" not only in political terms, but upon herself.[131] Her father and brother would do whatever they would to her, and those she loved, in order to fulfill their ambitions. In their eyes, her life was not hers to live, but theirs to shape. Recognizing that as long as she stayed in the sphere of their influence she would be a movable piece in play, she began to discern how she wanted to live. It was here that Lucrezia's relationship to the Kore emerged, a connection that shaped the next critical chapter of her life.

Toward the end of 1500, discussions for a marriage to Alfonso d'Este of Ferrara began. Ferrara was a powerful, old, aristocratic state in Italy. While the Papacy was influential, particularly in terms of spiritual authority, at that time Italy was still composed of individual states that were both financially and politically autonomous. The Pope wanted an alliance with the d'Este family because it would elevate the Borgias into the ranks of nobility. For Lucrezia, becoming Duchess of Ferrara would put her beyond the reach of her father and brother's influence because of Ferrara's independence and power. The d'Estes, however, were not keen on the alliance and despite attempts to wriggle out of it, political pressure was applied on several fronts, including the prospect of becoming a conquest in one of Cesare's military campaigns. In the late summer of 1501 while the Pope was touring new properties, Lucrezia was appointed Regent in charge of administrating at the Vatican, a position she held on a number of occasions.[132] The timing was fortunate for her as it coincided with discussions for the d'Este marriage, which meant she was directly involved in the negotiation of its terms. In the course of these discussions, Lucrezia developed a relationship with her future father-in-law out from under her father's influence, and this seems to have been a critical factor for victory. The marriage terms successfully negotiated, in February 1502 Lucrezia entered Ferrara in her bridal procession riding beneath a white silk canopy carried by the city's famed University professors.

In her new life in Ferrara, Lucrezia appears to have finally stepped out from the shadowy intrigues that surrounded her in Rome. Historians describe how over time she made a place for herself through patience, kindness, and graciousness, and all the d'Este family came to love her (the one exception being her legendary sister-in-law Isabella d'Este). While the first half of Lucrezia's life was defined by political power, and as Duchess of Ferrara she was responsible to political and civic duty, these were parts required of her, and were not related to her own needs of character. Lucrezia did not appear to seek control over others, neither fame or increase at anyone's expense, nor did she identify with the roles that were expected of one in her position. In Ferrara, she was neither passive, nor a mirror of whatever agenda the men in her life were pursuing. She retained her own tastes and she had no interest in pleasing others, but to be in company where she could be herself.[133] The poet Pietro Bembo, both her friend and lover, penned a dedication to Lucrezia for his work *Asolani*, which offers this insight into her nature, "She loves much more to please herself within than to please others without."[134] At her court in Ferrara, poets called her "most beautiful virgin."[135] She was described as having a "rare self-possession,"[136] which Bembo encouraged her to hold fast to when she was grieving her father's sudden death. She was the sole champion of her brother, whom she loved despite their violent history. Loyal and steadfast, her actions were an outgrowth of her nature, an expression of her values of charity, devotion, and religious piety. Her contemporaries described her as charming, sage, reticent, and elusive, and that hers was a "remote and solitary nature"[137]—something we can now identify as belonging to anyone in touch with the Kore archetype.

Enclosed and Pure

Any archetype lived in a one-sided way can become psychologically extreme. We all know spiritual adherents who fail to grow or thrive when practicing one-sided interiority, and we don't have to strain our mind's eye to find depictions of this aspect. In the fenced-in garden of the Virgin depicted in the Flemish Unicorn tapestries, or the Lady of Shallot who weaves night and day in her tower high above the ground, the Kore's shadow is easily identified—untouchable, impenetrable, self-enclosed.

One of the ways this chaste enclosure expresses itself is in an excessive concern with purity. Whenever we resist being affected by influences outside ourselves, it is this aspect of the Kore that is present. Kore resistance is at work when we're defended against another's point of view and unable to take in what they are sharing. This can extend to avoiding relationships because of what we fear they will require of us.

Believing oneself incorruptible by the forces of change that pervade life, we resist in order to remain innocent. It may appear in our attempts to withstand the deeper currents of change the psyche is calling for in favor of what we know and how we are managing things. Instead of opening to the changes, we stick to the well worn grooves of behavior or thought which keep us sealed off from meeting the inner tensions that generate energy and facilitiate psychological transformation. This need for stability can emerge in our attempt to remain untouched by life's turmoils and conflicts, unsullied by the chaos, messiness, and despair of the world. Too much of the Kore and one is closed off from life.

Hippolytus, son of the hero Theseus, shows us the resistance that belongs to this archetype through his devotion to purity. Dedicated to the Virgin goddess Artemis, he refuses Aphrodite and the entanglements of erotic love. By exclusively worshipping one divinity he becomes a target for divine wrath and Aphrodite makes him the unreceptive object of his step-mother's illicit passion, which leads to his death. In psychological terms, when we are dedicated solely to one set of principles, regardless of their merit, we are caught in a Hippolytian fixity that resists development. The Kore's purity, which is a spiritual quality of the archetype, is a part of her shadow configuration.

Hippolytus's rejection of Aphrodite's claims in favor of his conscious value, Artemisian virginity, is analogous to how we reject the psyche's otherness and its autonomy. In this vein, archetypal psychologist Pat Berry discusses how the psychic virgin is the one who resists the imagistic psyche and its communications in fantasy and dream images, the "psychic virgin is…closed to the image."[138] When we refrain from looking within to become conscious of the images that are the roots of our behaviors, we are defended against the psyche and closed off from its encircling presence. This clinging to our conscious value at the cost of deepening awareness of our interior plurality is a kind of Kore self-enclosure. It is by paying attention to other values—the many gods—that allows for the fullness life wants. In Jung's words, "To round itself out, life calls not for perfection but for completeness."[139]

Because the psychologically impenetrable one is closed off and therefore uninitiated into life, innocence itself is the shadow. Pamela Tait gives voice to this dusky side of the Kore, "To be innocent is to be 'not guilty.' You're not guilty because you haven't *done* anything, or at least nothing serious. I've learned to recognize the warning that the Kore is present when I experience her wide-eyed outrage: '*I don't deserve this! I haven't done anything wrong, why is this happening to me*?!'"[140] This cri de coeur reveals the sheltered in innocence part of us that only sees in terms of its blamelessness. Not having done anything, how could we have done anything wrong? When we are seeing through the pure eyes of the Kore, Persephone didn't deserve what happened to her. She should never have been abducted by Hades, never left her mother's side, and so remained the nameless girl untouched by loss and love, knowing nothing of the inner world that emerges only in solitude, or how psychological sovereignty is the result of living deeply into those experiences.

When we can embrace a more complex perspective that is not primarily concerned with maintaining psychological innocence, Persephone's myth shows us how Kore consciousness is forged by underworld initiations. It is in this realm that the shadowy experiences of loss, depression, and disconnection reveal and develop the soul's affinity for depth. Hillman's focus on how suffering belongs to the soul, what he calls pathologizing, helps us understand this aspect of the archetype. As a mode of imagining that is intrinsic to the psyche, pathologizing has us recognize that suffering is not an aberrant experience, rather it is archetypal and deeply human. The gods of the archetypal imagination enter life through our suffering, therefore, "by reverting the pathology to the God, we recognize the divinity of pathology and give the God his due."[141] Not only are the gods restored to psychology by imagining into our symptoms, their complexity (which is the soul's complexity) is more fully apprehended. Persephone–Kore is the divinity within the painful loss of innocence for it is she who shows how there would be no growing down into authenticity without the forays into the underworld. In this way we see the other archetypal dynamic at work, that where there is an excessive Kore enclosure, the forces on the side constellate experiences that carry the seeds of change.

**

The qualities the Kore personifies—unto-oneselfness, sovereignty, vitality—are archetypal ideals, and as such they feel sacred, even holy. This makes imagining how and where we can invite the Kore and live these aspects fraught with judgment. It is easy to slip into a way of thinking that harbors the belief that the Kore can only live in the most pure spaces of our life. Youth is one such place of imagining that carries a sense of unsullied wholeness, where we see in our younger selves the innocence and fierce potential that marks the Kore's presence. It is the feeling that she belongs to periods where we were still untouched by the harsh realities of life and had not yet come face to face with our difficult complexes which seem to only harden with age. Another way we relegate this figure is by thinking that our Kore nature will be able to thrive only once we have gotten it all together and are free and clear of old issues and wounds. Both these sketches are variations on the idea that we must be fixed, clean, or pure in order to receive the Kore. Perhaps we think korehood impossible because we are too much shaped by sociocultural challenges or family tragedies and responsibilities that preclude the possibility of stepping into the space of vitality and possibility she personifies. In other words, we believe ourselves denied access to those sacred pools in which korehood can be renewed. All these ways of thinking about the problem of being in relationship to the Kore share the idea that she is somehow separate from life, belonging to some pristine area of pure grace.

I believe these errors of vision, which are honestly made, is partly due to the numinous energy of the Kore. After all, the teleology of the soul is towards korehood. While that is a psychological reality described by Jung as individuation and symbolized by the inner image of divinity he called the Self, it also means accurately seeing our relationship to this soulmaking process is inherently difficult. One of the oldest surviving Hermetic texts, *Kore Kosmou* or *The Virgin of the World*, comes to assist us in correcting these mistakes in our perception. In this text, Persephone-Kore symbolizes the soul:

> Wherefore, considered as the daughter of Zeus and Demeter, Kore is immaculate and celestial in character; considered as the captive and consort of Hades, she belongs to the lower world and to the region of lamentation and dissolution. And, indeed, the Soul possesses the dual nature thus ascribed to her, for she is in her interior and proper quality, incorrupt and inviolable—ever virgin—while in her apparent and relative quality, she is defiled and fallen.[142]

Mythically, the celestial Kore and the fallen Kore are distinct. However, in life there is a classical young Kore period, but that quality can be lived all throughout life. The Hermetic wisdom says life, by definition, is about contamination. We get wounded. Being of earth, our condition is of organic matter and its inexorable laws of time. We get dirty in the mess of living, and yet there is this archetypal quality of soul that can remain pure in the midst of that. Psychologically speaking, the celestial Kore and the fallen Kore are one and the same, aspects of a single archetypal pattern. It is the fallen aspect that makes possible recognition of the celestial, or we could say, the divine needs the broken. In the words of W. B Yeats:

> But Love has pitched his mansion in
> The place of excrement
> For nothing can be sole or whole
> That has not been rent.[143]

This idea of the purity of the soul in the matter of life is very much in line with how Irigaray defines virginity as "a woman's possession, a natural and spiritual possession to which she has a right and for which she holds responsibilities."[144] In other words, virginity is a psychological attitude born from living deeply into the matters of life. We can always return, no matter our condition or age, to draw water from the Kore's spring. It is she who guides our imagining into those qualities of beingness that are connected to the vivifying waters of the spirit. We can allow these archetypal patterns to remain suspended above life, but our task really is to bring them down into the world of being and create an ensoulment. For Jung, this is also what individuation is about.

> Individuation is not an intensification of consciousness, it
> is very much more. For you must have the consciousness
> of something before it can be intensified, and that means
> experience, life lived. You can only be really conscious of
> things which you have experienced, so individuation must
> be understood as life. Only life integrates, only life and
> what we do in life makes the individual appear. You cannot

individuate, for instance, by locking yourself up in a cell, you can only individuate in your concrete life, you appear in your deed; there you can individuate and nowhere else. Real consciousness can only be based upon life; upon things experienced, but talking about these things is just air. It is a sort of conscious understanding, but it is not individuation. Individuation is the accomplishment through life. For instance, say a cell begins to divide itself and to differentiate and develop into a certain plant or a certain animal; that is the process of individuation. It is that one becomes what one is, that one accomplishes one's destiny, all the determinations that are given in the form of the germ; it is the unfolding of the germ and becoming the primitive pattern that one was both with.[145]

Returning to the idea that the Kore personifies the Self, that imaginal figure at work in the dynamic process of individuation, for ensoulment to be vesseled in life one is obliged to embrace the heavenly, earthy and underworld aspects. The archetype can only be realized in the totality of being.

∗∗∗

Boundaries, whether physical, psychological, or emotional, are expressions of Kore enclosure. Artemis, as the goddess who comes from afar, helps us understand how the Kore conceals herself. "The Virgin Artemis," writes Paris, is the "archetype of a femininity that is pure and primitive."[146] By primitive, Paris means close to the animal, and this aspect of the Kore whose feet are rooted in the natural world stands in contrast to civilization and its values as personified by Athena. In Homer, Artemis is called *hagne*, a designation that combines "holy" and "pure," which Otto notes is frequently applied to the untouched aspects of nature, such as virgin forests.[147] Artemis signifies those parts of our own nature that defy civilized structures, its relational laws and instinct sublimating processes.

Thus Artemis, says Paris, "comes to sanctify solitude, natural and primitive living to which we may all return whenever we find it necessary to belong only to ourselves. An Amazon and infallible archer, Artemis guarantees our resistance to a domestication that would be too complete."[148]

As Goddess of the wild life of the woods, all animals of forest and field are sacred to her including lions, boars, stags, wolves, bears and quail.[149] Attending the birth of animals as divine midwife, Artemis also participates in their death with her bows and arrows in the hunt, which is her particular game of pleasure. We see then that her character combines the natural rhythms of life and death that underly all Nature. These seemingly incongruent aspects—the purity and solitude of the Kore and the Mother-Midwife—are dual aspects of this goddess.

FIGURE 6. ARTEMIS AS MISTRESS OF BEASTS
(BLACK-FIGURE VASE, ARCHAIC, GREECE, C. 570 B.C.)

Arcadia, Artemis's realm, is an ever-distant wilderness whose remoteness from both the gods and humans make it a boundary within which she resides in solitude. This landscape of seclusion that invites aloneness corresponds to her virginity. The oldest surviving archaic Kore statue in the world testifies to the distance that is so characteristic of Artemis. Made as an offering to the goddess, its inscription bears its dedication by Nikandre of Naxos to "the far darting one, the lover of the bow."[150] This archeological treasure shows how even in terms of space and time, to Artemis belongs what is remote.

Artemis personifies a force that enjoins us to build the psychological defenses that protect us from negative influences or inappropriate incursions. From this vantage point, the exclusivity of Hippolytus' devotion to Artemis is the capacity to defend sacred territory. In one version of his myth, she rescues him right before his death and brings him to a sacred forest where he builds a temple to her. Paris describes his second life:

> This priest of Artemis kept his place until a successor took it from him by killing him. The hermit had, therefore, to exercise an extreme vigilance, for at the same time as he preserved the forest of Artemis from intrusion, he was protecting his own life. In this I see an illustration of a rather frequent psychological situation, that is, the necessity of repulsing the invader, even violently. Whoever wishes to know solitude should protect himself or herself from any kind of intrusion, physical or psychological, and the person who too easily opens his arms, without demarcating the unapproachable ground, cannot know of Artemis.[151]

At certain times it may be necessary to be closed off from the influences of the world and other people. Artists, writers and scholars all know the necessity of solitude, their closed doors a boundary marker which must be respected in order to create. So too at those significant periods in life marked by crisis and change, one must retreat on some level from the usual busy-ness of the world in order to turn inward and listen into what is trying to emerge in awareness. At these times, solitude is necessary. The

Kore shows how knowing when and how to be impregnable to another's influence so the integrity of one's developing awareness can be maintained. Knowing Artemis means coming to know the necessity of boundaries.

✱✱✱

A great sorceress, Circe is an herbalist and spell-crafter who lives alone on her own island. Circe is the root of *circle* and comes from the feminine form of the Greek *kirkos* which Kerényi connects to the, "circling birds of prey...circling ambulation of the wolf and in Homer the hawk."[152] In other words, Circe's is an encircling consciousness. This is the basis of magic rituals which are most often made in a circle, drawn to consecrate the time and space in which the powers are raised and dispersed. It's the creation of an enclosed and sacred space, a world within the world. Circe and the encircling motions of her magical arts on her solitary island engirdled by the sea illustrate the encompassing containment of Kore consciousness.

Among Circe's craft are spells and enchantments which gives her the power to bind others to her will. When Odysseus arrives on her island, she turns his hapless crew into pigs. He himself escapes this humbling metamorphosis because he was forewarned by Hermes of her proclivity to work magic on uninvited visitors and given a special herb to protect him from her magic. But Odysseus is not immune to all of Circe's powers. There was no herb offered to shield him from the enchantments that belong to Aphrodite's grimorie, and he becomes Circe's lover.

The animal motif that rings around Circe suggests a connection to Artemis, whose epithet 'Lady of the Wild Beasts' reminds us how she works to keep us connected to our animal primitivity. Circe and Artemis personify this wild, magic aspect of consciousness that is rooted in the natural world far from the forces of civilization and human society. And yet, despite their proclivity for solitude, there are times when both share in the company of others. This conveys something of the tension that the dual needs for solitude and intimacy engender. Circe hosts Odysseus on her island and takes him to her bed. With Artemis, her love of the Arcadian wilderness and the solitary pleasures of the hunt is matched only by her love of dancing with the Graces and Muses.

Transgression

Greek myths depict the archetypal principles that emerge at the crossroads of the primitive and the civilized. The figures personify deep psychological processes that involve the collision between deep instincts including proclivities toward violence and aggression, and our culture-making tendencies. This is why myths include difficult motifs such as infanticide, rape, war and other experiences we prefer not to look at. On the psychological level, these horrific images force us to recognize that we cannot sentimentalize the psyche. We encounter shadow figures in our lives with difficulty and repulsion, and some of our instincts are not aligned with what belongs to civilized life. Having looked at the light and dark sides of the Kore's enclosure and purity, we now need to consider one such motif that constellates around this figure. Wherever the Kore appears we find there are forces that attempt to infringe upon her boundaries, which shows how, archetypally speaking, excessive purity constellates the prospect of violent ravishment.

Artemis in particular personifies this dynamic of transgression that dogs the heels of what is virginal. While bathing in a pool in her Arcadian wilderness, Artemis is assailed by the gaze of the unwitting hunter Actaeon when he becomes lost in her woods. Furious that she has been seen naked, penetrated by the eyes of a mortal no less, she turns him into a stag. Having undergone this metamorphosis, Actaeon is unrecognized by his hounds, and they tear him apart. The nymph Callisto, beloved companion of Artemis, suffers a similar fate. Under secrecy Callisto becomes Zeus's lover, and is soon pregnant and unable to hide her growing belly. When Artemis sees Callisto's changing form while they bathe, she is mad with betrayal and in her fury transforms her into a she-bear. Again we see Artemis responding violently to incursions upon the purity of her world, personified by masculine figures both mortal and divine. The difference in

Athena

this tale is that the punishment is carried by someone Artemis loves, and in grief for the loss of her friend, she turns Callisto into the constellation of the bear, Ursa Major, where she remains visible from a cool distance. Nonetheless, the vengeance of the Virgin is total.

This issue of the Kore's self-containment constellating transgression can also be seen at work in the myth of Medusa and Athena, though with a particular twist. Unlike Artemis, who in doing away with the perpetrators restores the integrity of her world, Athena comes to bear the face of the violation as a part of herself, which helps us imagine into how violation and sovereignty also belong to the archetypal configuration of the Kore.

Athena's temple is desecrated by Poseidon when he rapes Medusa, a beautiful mortal, within its walls. Furious that her sacred grounds were defiled, she punishes Medusa by turning her into a Gorgon with writhing snakes for hair and eyes that can turn any living creature to stone.[153] Medusa becomes deadly unapproachable, a shadow Kore figure protected from further transgression, and she herself now capable of violent penetration through the eyes. This scene compels us to recognize how Athena's reaction to Medusa is an image of how impersonal the objective psyche can be sometimes. It is like coming across a wild animal in nature—we can end up in the wrong place at the wrong time and innocently violate a principle. In this sense, Medusa is a tragic figure because though taken against her will by one divinity, she nonetheless transgresses the principles belonging to another.

Like the myth of Persephone and Demeter, Medusa and Athena are often discussed on a sociological and personalistic level, thus Medusa's rape becomes an allegory of patriarchal power and abuse, and Athena's actions become a morality play on female power, betrayal and cruelty. While there is a place for these interpretative valences, something important is lost when myth is read in these terms rather than metaphorically. We start looking at these figures as human beings with lives rather than interrelated principles and propensities. From an archetypal perspective, Medusa's violation is intrinsic to Athena's Kore nature. The mythic figures show us the raw patterns and energetic collisions, and our task is to awaken to these and neither unconsciously identify with them or naively escape them.

In order to go deeper into the configuration of Medusa and Athena, and what that has to do with the theme of violation and the Kore, Hillman's treatment of Persephone provides valuable clues. For Hillman, Persephone is an image of the soul being initiated into the psyche through its descent into the underworld of the psyche. This movement down breaks open the innocent ego to the symbolic and pluralistic realm that lives beneath our day-world consciousness. Persephone, he writes, "represents this movement of the soul from defense against Hades to love for him."[154] That is, Persephone as soul-aware consciousness comes to love the psyche's depths and darkness, its proclivities toward suffering, and the cycles of death and renewal that are intrinsic to life. It is in this movement that Persephone becomes queen. Medusa, whose names means "Queen" and "Guardian," is another mythic image of the soul initiated through descent. The strange detail of her mortality in contrast to her Gorgon sister's immortality begins to make sense when approached from this perspective. Being mortal means being vulnerable to the will of the gods, who come in various guises such as illness, loss, age, and death.

Both Medusa and Athena are violated, and this configuration repeats itself in myth over and again, because archetypally, solitude and virginity constellate its opposite. Unto-herself, it is the Kore's virginal containment and inaccessibility that attracts that which wants to be joined with it. That which resists access becomes that which is most desired: the nymph Daphne fleeing Apollo's embrace, Cassandra cursed with Apollo's gift, Persephone caught up in Hades' arms, Thetis's transformative resistance to Peleus all illustrate this dynamic.

Intrinsic then to the archetypal configuration of the Kore are experiences of violation. This, in no way, is a legitimization of literal rape. What it does mean is that psychological violation and psychological sovereignty are connected, for sovereignty only emerges out of an urgent need for agency. When we don't know the value of our psychic boundaries or where they lie, these are the very conditions that lead to their testing and transgression. Lucrezia Borgia exemplified this the first twenty years of her life. Knowing what belongs within the walls of one's psychic house, what lines requires defense, belong to the Athenian face of the Kore.

Sometime after Medusa's metamorphosis the hero Perseus is tasked by King Polydektes to acquire her head. Perseus is aided in his task by Athena, and he travels to the island of the Graiai, the Gorgon's sisters, because only they know where Medusa is to be found. By stealing their one eye, Perseus forces the Graiai to reveal her location and through uncharted territories he makes his way to the Gorgon's home where he waits for Medusa to fall asleep and then kills her. At the end of Perseus's adventure, Athena demands Medusa's head be brought to her so that she can affix it to her breastplate. Medusa's head, called the *gorgoneion*, becomes Athena's crest, a visual signature by which the goddess is immediately recognizable. This image is deeply ingrained in our cultural mind's eye, so much so that we cannot know Athena without Medusa's head emblazoned upon her breast. Athena's armor guarantees her purity, and it is precisely what requires the dark face of the Kore to emerge in her sphere. In essence, Medusa becomes Athena's other face, her shadow sister, connecting Athena to the violation that is an intrinsic part of the Kore pattern. To embrace the full nature of Athena, we cannot do without Medusa. The entire spectrum of this archetypal configuration from the light to the dark, belongs to the Kore pattern.

CHAPTER FIVE

Spirited Agency

All Kore statues, the diminutive ones that were placed on altars and the huge Caryatids that bear the weight of Athena's temple at the Acropolis, stand erect. Nowhere have there been found sitting or reclining Korai. Their striking characteristic stance communicates straightforwardness, strength, and presence. As though filled with the sap of life, these figures undulate with energy. In this vein, it's hard to overlook the phallic countenance in this erect stature of the Korai statues. How the archetypal phallos, an assertive force, appears in the psychology of the Kore deserves consideration.

Conveying vitality, the Kore stands erect in the world. The ubiquitous presence of the Kore in archaic and classical Greek religion shows how she puts herself forth, taking a stance in relationship to the culture. In psychological terms, korehood does not mean waiting to be seeded but approaches life with a receptive openness and expectation. Neither static nor passive, Kore erectness is active beingness. This vigorous dynamism is distinct in Athena whose epithet Pallas, "suggests a robust, fierce maidenliness," which Kerényi characterizes as a "distinct masculinity."[155] With Artemis we saw the ferocity that is turned upon intruders and companions alike in defense of her virginal territory. This lightning quick responsiveness mirrors the phallos, whose arousal is easily evoked. In the cult festival of Artemis in Korythalia the goddess was worshipped by women who attached huge phalli to their costumes for ritual dancing.[156] It is Artemis who nurtures our ability to be aggressively alert and responsive to presences in our environment.

The Kore's ability to encompass the archetypal phallos and its erect vitality gives her a special connection to what I call spirited agency. Extolling individuality, the Kore stands apart from others. Having looked at Kore individuality and her capacity to stand her ground, here I want to amplify these themes in what I call the accoutrements of independence.

Historically, female adolescent fire has been insufficiently imagined in our culture. Because we haven't had images for this quality and its enduring archetypal pattern, it has very often been misunderstood, stereotyped, and repressed. Young girls who enjoy physical activities, wearing roomier boys clothes, refusing barrettes, and having their hair tamed used to be called tomboys, a term colored by connotations of rudeness and impropriety. While being a tomboy may be tolerated when girls are young, when they become teenagers the display of "masculine" traits can be judged as defiance of gender roles. The assumption that girls are, or should be, more relationship-oriented is often a tacit rule that when not conformed to is translated as rebellion. And what has been read as rebellion in young women has often seen as initiative and independence in young men.

As a young goddess Artemis rejected "womanly" expectations, choosing as she did to remain unmarried, wear a hunting dress, and live free from the social expectations and constraints of Olympus, the civilized world of the gods. Those archetypally Artemisian things that claim independence and are related to something intrinsic like nature and animals, or the desire to be with one's wild gang and beyond the parents, have often been judged by society. Can our culture with its lack of differentiated consciousness know the difference between korehood and rebellion? Tomboys and rebels are stereotypes, and as such are incapable of opening into the deeper archetypal patterns that lie within these behaviors and values. To take a cue from Hillman, who argued that depression looks the way it does because of our manic culture and its inability to differentiate it from melancholy, perhaps a young woman's korehood looks like rebellion because of the way it sits in patriarchal culture.

Kore assertiveness is an energy that drives cultural transformation. In 1989 a group of young women defied the male dominated sailing world and crewed their own yacht in the Whitbread Race around the world. Their vessel was named Maiden, and it was the first all women crew to enter a professional sailing race. In the story of the Maiden crew, one hears an old tale—the resistance to women participating in a field because 'girls don't do that.' The Maiden was rejected by hundreds of corporate sponsors, and the crew often belittled and trivialized by the media. In spite of the challenges, Tracy Edwards's ambitious vision and the solidarity of the crew she assembled broke through the resistances that work to keep women in their traditional places and out of the wider world. Because of their strength, skill and defiant spirit, the Maiden became the most beloved ship of the race.

Kore female adolescent fire is the strength *to be*, whether it looks like an Artemisian tomboy or an Athenian leader in-the-making. What looks like rebellion on the outside is a declaration of identity in opposition to the traditional values that family and society adhere to. In adolescent girls, this sense of self is there in potential. We've all known girls who have a groundedness that seems beyond their years, those who defy their age by the seriousness of their concerns. Ligaya Mishan describes a photo of the young climate activist Greta Thurnberg who cut school to protest, "sitting alone, a wan, forlorn looking 15-year-old with braids, beside her hot pink backpack (a totem of girlhood) on the cobblestones outside the Swedish Parliament in Stockholm."[157] There is Wynta-Amor Rogers, the 7-year-old who was captured on video, "chanting 'No justice, no peace' and shaking a stern finger at a protest over the police killing of George Floyd...There is something of the prodigy in her extraordinary poise and conviction, but also defiance of any lingering stereotype that girls are fragile," reflects Mishan. These images have become engrained in our cultural parlance, and it is critical that we can identify this juxtaposition of youth and gravitas, as well as boldness of spirit, as belonging to the Kore. We need to know the archetypal pattern at work so we can bring it further into consciousness.

One of the most beloved novels about a Kore claimed girl is *Anne of Green Gables*, written by Canadian author Lucy Maud Montgomery at the turn of the 20th century. An orphan, Anne is adopted by the Marilla and John Cuthbert, aged siblings whose house is the eponymous Green Gables. In her first few days Anne meets Mrs. Lind, the exacerbating busybody who is Marilla's friend and neighbor. Mrs. Lind is scandalized by the adoption, and upon meeting Anne she takes liberties to comment on her appearance, calling her ugly and skinny, with hair "as red as carrots."[158] Refusing to silently absorb insult and belittlement, and with no apparent fear of losing the home she has only so tenuously inhabited, Anne's personal integrity matters more than being a well-mannered girl. Though she needs a home and a sense of belonging more than anything, she will not abdicate her self-regard for it, and Anne responds with an outburst of temper. This refusal to betray herself simply because someone expects something of her is the erect Kore. It is the fertilizing thrust into life of the archetypal phallos that says I AM, and is rooted in the ground of her being. I AM, says the Kore and she expects the world to receive her.

Despite Anne's fiery behavior and the fuss she makes about apologizing, Marilla loves Anne all the more. This remarkable acceptance cuts to the quick the toxic belief that to be loved one has to be pleasing. Anne is loved not because she pleases, she is loved because she is herself, and in being herself she pleases. Her self-worth which she fiercely defends is not a thinly concealed egoic pride. Having been an orphan her entire life she wants to belong and develop meaningful relationships. Time and time again we see Anne apologize for her mistakes, whether saying something that inadvertently offends another, or when her actions lead to disastrously funny situations.

Kore fire appears in the symbolism belonging to the cult worship of Artemis at Brauron (one of the twelve cities of ancient Attica). It was the religious custom to dedicate young girls, around the age of 9 years old, to Artemis at her temple for a period of time before marriage. The initiation into the cult occurred every five years at the Festival of Brauronia, where girls in saffron-colored robes called *krokoton*, Greek for the crocus flower from which saffron is harvested, were consecrated to the goddess. During their time in service to the goddess, the girls were called *arktoi* "she-bears." Their bearhood was in essence an Artemisian korehood, a period that Paris says was marked by the girls being allowed to hunt, play physical games, and enjoy all the freedoms that boys of the same age were accorded in Greek patriarchal society.[159] Kerenyi describes how in their ritual processions, "dressed in the krokoton, to serve the maiden Goddess, the Athenian young girl was herself like a bright flame."[160] Whether real-life persons, mythic or literary characters, these girls suffused with the fire of the Kore, capture something, reminding us of that part of ourselves that flamed in our youth. The longing we often feel for reconnection to this part of ourselves reveals how the soul longs for korehood.

***

Music, like poetry, makes the gods palpable. In Tori Amos' work, the Kore steps forward with extraordinary clarity. One of the themes that appears over and again in Amos' oeuvre is the forging of one's autonomy and creativity as a woman. The quest for freedom from both inner and outer ideologies of control is a river of fire running through her albums. These concerns are rooted in her childhood to which she often refers back, particularly to her paternal grandmother who Amos calls her "greatest adversary and challenger" because of her puritanical and dogmatic Christianity which upheld the subordination of women to men and the rule of God the Father.[161]

Amos recounts the religious atmosphere of her childhood home as one that was suffused with "the need to control…the need to dominate by subjugating others so they believe in your God, in your way."[162]

Masquerading as Christian values, her grandmother exercised dominance, control, and aggression. Amos says, "Where is emancipation in this kind of spiritual bullying? At five I knew I was at war with my grandmother…If a woman wanting to choose her own path, sexually and spiritually, went against Grandmother's puritanical belief system, then she would be treated…as a pariah. This made me close ranks within my Being. Close ranks…[against] my grandmother's methodology and orthodoxy."[163] Even at a young age, some people know what is poison to their system. In Amos's case, this difficult relationship created the conditions for the emergence of Kore consciousness. We are confronted again with the archetypal pairing of violation and korehood. The transgression of one's deep values, which is one's virginal nature, is paradoxically the wounding experience that can constellate the forces of defense. Like the Kore who reject their pursuers or Artemis who destroys the perpetrators of her sacred spring, Amos resisted these ideological onslaughts by making aspects of herself inviolable.

The early emergence of a sense of sovereignty that Amos describes was born from these injurious experiences of judgment. In refusing her grandmother's convictions, she sealed herself off from patriarchal Christianity, rejecting its violent incursions. Amos realized she had to find another way to be and connect with others. Interestingly, this leads Amos to reflect on the issue of penetration. She asks, "How does a woman penetrate? It's a beautiful paradox."[164] How does a woman assert herself without wielding the archetypal phallos in a patriarchal way? The answer is in the image of the Kore and her phallic uprightness. The efficacy of the archetypal phallos as it moves through the Kore is at work when a woman relates to life out of her sense of what matters to her, thereby penetrating the ground of being. The Kore's embrace of the phallos is the ability to relate from one's matter, and this generates a feeling of agency. The connection to one's inner terrain makes viable the psychological ground one needs to inhabit one's life and move effectively within it.

For Amos, the question of how a woman penetrates also has to do with demarcation, "That word [penetrate] now is really about an opening, an entering into separate space...I realized that it was okay to enter that space without having to be invaded."[165] Abiding within oneself without having to let others in is, at times, absolutely necessary. We need psychic boundaries, and these are created only when we have a sufficient sense of self to delineate what is ours and what's not. The struggle in this process of discernment is expressed by Amos in her song "Take to the Sky," whose rhythm is punctuated by deep drumbeats. The lyrics tell of the onslaught of criticism from the authority figures in her life—father, priest, and doctor. In the first few lines she describes their cutting remarks about what she isn't doing right with her life, and how her attempts at escape are thwarted by her heart bound sense of duty to the world of the Father. Despite these pressures, she comes to wield a sword, an instrument of discernment that allows her to separate her truth from those external judgments. Compelled by the Kore's spirited agency, Amos, with her fiery red mane, takes hold of the sword and takes to the sky.

Youthfulness

Kore youthfulness is characterized by newness and possibility. Its constellation rises at the birth of spring when seeds begin bursting into tender shoots, vibrant green, shivering with the sap of life. Possibility is intrinsic to new life, as the seed destined to unfold over time and fulfill its potential; bud becomes thousand-petalled peony, tiny acorn becomes oak, slender new moon becomes gravid with light.

Eternally youthful, all Kore statues have soft round features, their brows unmarked by lines of concern and age. Their small high breasts and slender waists are those of young women who have not carried children, and their long unbound hair indicates they are unmarried.

FIGURE 7. AKROPOLIS KORE WITH SERPENTINE DIADEM
(MARBLE, ARCHAIC, GREECE, C. 520 B.C.)

Wearing a serpentine diadem, her smooth skin glows across the strong planes of her face, her cheeks flushed with life (figure 7). Her distinctive smile lifts everything up, expressing pleasure. Her left arm, encircled by a bracelet and lifting a fold of her long dress (*paryphe*) is sinuous and graceful.

FIGURE 8. AKROPOLIS KORE WITH BEEHIVE HAIR
(MARBLE, ARCHAIC, GREECE, C. 525 B.C.)

The round, spring moon face of the Kore with the beehive hair glows (figure 8). Her stoic gaze leveled straight ahead conveys a disimpassioned interest in what is occurring around her. More serious than her sister, her full lips are pursed on the edge of a smile. Her stiff posture suggests a formality in her nature, perhaps pride in both her beauty and position.

For all the individuality these statues convey, they invite an exploration of the significance of youth and how that relates to the archetypal field of the Kore. Youthfulness is one of the primary features of all Kore, statues and mythic figures alike, and when we consider how and where this sits in the psyche we recognize its profound place in the imagination. Youthfulness and youthful phases of life are haunting; they stay with us, and our psyches return to them again and again. It's a place of new sparks, landscapes of reimagining, where possibility is a source of renewal. Like Persephone, who in reemerging from Hades each year in the springtime is in essence reborn, the Kore points to the renewal that lives within juvenescent images of the psyche.

As a psychological quality, youthfulness is related to originality and freshness. Thus contact with the Kore means things never get old. She brings a springtime perspective and revives imagination. The Kore spirit can be seen in those experiences we have when an air of possibility arises like a fresh breeze that carries on it new thoughts and feelings. The virginal psyche seeks, Thomas Moore writes, "a new attitude, a fresh perspective, a new image, or even a familiar image freshly reimagined."[166]

It is the bright-eyed Kore that seeks the spark of potential in life, murmuring as Anne of Green Gables does, "tomorrow is always fresh, with no mistakes in it."[167] Anne's imagination is a bubbling spring, her fantasy life a means of protection from the brutal realities she faced as an orphan (she was three months old when she was sent to an orphanage). But it would be wrong to reduce her imagination to a mechanism for survival, a mere tool for coping; for imaginative play is how Anne opens up to the world and its possibilities. Anne shows us how the life of the spirit requires imagination, and the soul requires beauty. Combining tenderness and vulnerability with fresh vigor, Kore youthfulness is the essence of new life.

The joy Anne brings to her foster mother Marilla comes from her ability to awaken in her a feeling for the new and unexpected. Startlingly insightful, Anne often sees into the essence of things which she stumbles upon simply by stating what she sees or how something makes her feel. Her lack of any consistent education, either scholastic, moral, or religious (she imagines prayer as something one feels while gazing at the sky at night in a grove of trees, which is downright scandalous to Marilla), is what preserved this freshness, that little bit of wildness which is so much a part of her nature. The lines of Browning's that L. M. Montgomery chose as the epigraph for the book, Anne's christening if you will, captures this elemental spiritedness, "The good stars met in your horoscope/Made you of spirit and fire and dew."[168]

Barriers

—

CHAPTER SIX

The Great Mother Goddess

Identifying the mythic Kore and how she appears in life is one part of inviting this archetypal pattern into consciousness. Her reemergence also necessitates a second consideration, namely an inquiry into the forces that occlude this pattern. The main barriers to Kore consciousness are constructed by authority and power. The subversion of female power and sovereignty in patriarchal paradigms, with their one-sided systems of masculine hierarchical authority maintained through dominance, and often through violence, comprise one such barrier, and have been examined in great depth in various disciplines including women's studies, history, religious studies, gender and cultural studies. Here I want to turn our attention to a second authoritative power that is less often discussed coming from the other side of the spectrum—the Mother. Her domination of feminine ways of being constitutes the largest barrier to the Kore, and this hindrance needs attention. Let us look at the archetypal Mother's power and the particular problems it poses in relation to Kore consciousness.

There are two words that describe the spell the Mother can cast upon us—no escape. She personifies the very earth from which we come and to which we will return. She embraces the mysteries of both life and death in the sense of continuous fertility and renewal. The mothering field exerts a gravitational pull that is difficult to resist. To put it in positive terms, Mother is always there. To put it in negative terms, one way or another Mother never leaves.

The Mother archetype is a pervasive and foundational pattern in our lived experience. We begin life inside our mother and experience the surrounding womb environment as the source of life itself. Culturally, the image of nature's totality, the earth and its life sustaining conditions also pertain to the Mother pattern. The unconscious, as the source of consciousness, is also the Mother because we experience this as the deep matrix of psychological life. While consciousness obviously plays a critical part in the psyche, it is small in comparison to the psyche as a whole, which extends beyond the personal into the archaic archetypal structures that pattern all experience. These underlying powers are separate from the mind's conscious orientation, and understood as the more instinctive aspects of the psyche, Jung writes that they are carried into consciousness through images of the Mother.[169]

However, psychological awareness cannot occur by remaining within the instinctive sphere of the psyche. The precondition for consciousness is separation out of this primordial realm. Separation is likewise required on the outer relational level; our early life task is to detach from our personal mother to engage with life, because the "forward-striving libido which rules the conscious mind," writes Jung, "...demands separation from the mother."[170] Without some measure of detachment a child's potential can be suffocated and their development stifled. While the process of adaptation to new circumstances and the deepening into our character continues beyond childhood and throughout life, the problem we often face is an endurance of the Mother archetype in situations and stages of development where she no longer fulfills a fitting psychological role. For a woman attempting to come to terms with the Kore's claim on her psyche, and for a man relating to this aspect of his psychic being, the intrusion or pressure of the Mother archetype can be deleterious.

In *The Soul's Code,* James Hillman provides a stark example of this collision with the Mother archetype in the way we imagine our path through life. The parental fallacy, he says, is that omnipresent idea that our parents are the primary agents of our destiny and the architects of our lives. The parental fallacy is not just a problem of personal psychology, it is an archetypal fantasy too, for behind our personal mother sits the Great Mother. The cost of this perspective is that it makes us victims of a theory that gives the Great Mother power over us especially in a conspiracy of nature and nurture—that developmental binary that is also binding. Hillman offers a contrasting and ancient view, namely that children have their own fate, their own daimon or calling, and the challenge lies in recognizing "our individuality as a birthright without the fallback pillow of Mother as comforting ground and archetypal support."[171] Recognizing where the Mother archetype has taken hold of us (as in the idea of parents as dictators of fate) and seeing through it so that we can relate to our own unique calling, thus becomes a critical act of psychological maturation.

Aside from the foundational character of this pattern there may be other reasons our culture remains under the spell of the Great Mother. One is that we fail to see the archetypal world in any form, so we remain blind to the transpersonal forces that infuse and shape personal experience. In other words, for us to be able to appropriately pivot away from the Mother we must begin with a more conscious relation to her realm. In American culture in particular, because of the very narrow and limited ways in which we care for and nurture children, each other and the world around us, we rarify and idealize both the personal mother and mothering.

The problem of the Mother archetype as a barrier to individuality is perhaps more acute for women where the relationship with one's mother is intricately bound up with one's own identity as a woman. As psychoanalyst Nini Herman argues, woman's "growth and greater freedom are continually aborted in a subversive two-way traffic" [172] of the mother-daughter pair, which she identifies as an issue older and deeper than the patriarchal paradigm. The roots of the personal problem of the mother-daughter relationship are reflected in the archetypal dynamic of the Mother and the Kore.

In consciously reclaiming that aspect of soul that is apart from the parents, we can release the archetypal Mother's more unconscious claims on us and rediscover it in more fitting places in our life. The Mother archetype is not the problem as such, it's a matter of *how* and *where* she enters our lives. So it is behooving to become conscious of places where the Mother has worn out her welcome. Other archetypal patterns can then play a fundamental role in our psyches. If one's inner image of relating is dominated by the Mother, for example, it can be difficult for true intimacy to develop because very often one's own needs are set aside for the needs of the other. Paradoxically this gives one a sense of control as well as excessive responsibility. Compulsive caregiving does not make room for the openness and vulnerability required for authentic relationships, thereby making the shared responsibilities of such a connection very difficult.

***

Let's grasp the gravity of this archetypal pattern by hearing the Great Mother in her own words. In *Metamorphosis: the Golden Ass* from the late 2nd century AD, the goddess Isis appears to her initiate Lucius Apuleius and utters these words,

ISIS

> I am Nature, the universal Mother, mistress of all the elements, primordial child of time, sovereign of all things spiritual, queen of the dead, queen also of the immortals, the single manifestation of all gods and goddesses that are. My nod governs the shining heights of Heaven, the wholesome sea-breezes, the lamentable silences of the world below. Though I am worshipped in many aspects, known by countless names, and propitiated with all manner of different rites, yet the whole round earth venerates me.[173]

In Apuleius' vision, Isis expresses a religious order and image of divinity that predates the Roman Empire and reaches back to the Neolithic civilization of Old Europe (circa 7500-3500 BCE), which is the root system of all the primary symbols of Western myth and religion. As archaeomythologist Marija Gimbutas has shown, this was a settled and agricultural civilization that was matrilineal and egalitarian in social structure, bore no evidence of warfare, and its religious imagination included the worship of female as well as male divinities.[174] Thousands of marked figurines and other cult objects have been excavated in many Neolithic sites. The sheer number of female figurines in different materials including clay, stone, bone, ceramics, and various metals that Gimbutas studied is staggering—approximately 30,000 miniature sculptures from the Neolithic period from over 3,000 sites in southeastern Europe. Gimbutas argues that the specific visual symbolic language of the Neolithic is traceable through the early history of Europe and the Mediterranean and, "represent the grammar and syntax of a kind of meta-language by which an entire constellation of meanings is transmitted."[175]

Gimbutas' groundbreaking archeological and mythological studies reveal the Great Mother Goddess to be the primary deity of Neolithic civilization. The female figurines, many of which are anthropomorphic and zoomorphic, establishes the primacy of female divinity. Far fewer male figurines were found with no equivalent Father God figures, which for Gimbutas contributed to the "sovereignty of motherhood" in this civilization.[176] The Mother Goddess was the fruitful source of all life and her symbolism revolves around the mysteries of birth, death and renewal. The fundamental and underlying unity of Nature is revealed in the body of Great Goddess, who personified the "eternally renewing cycle of life in all of its forms and manifestations."[177] The paradox of unity and multiplicity is central to the Neolithic Great Mother Goddess, for while there are a great variety of figures expressing the array of life's forms and creative energies of the cosmos, the Great Goddess was the singular source of all life. Therefore, while we find her power inflected in three main faces—the Creatrix who brings forth life, the Death Goddess who takes life away, and the Regeneratrix who renews life, Gimbutas emphasizes unity as her essence, a point we will return to.

Many of the symbols that cluster around the Great Goddess as Life-Giving Creatrix exhibit the generative powers of nature and predominately belong to the aquatic sphere.[178] Water is the source of life, from the amniotic fluids at birth and the mother's breast, to the natural water ways, rivers, lakes and springs, it is essential for all living beings and human habitation. The body of the Goddess as the source of all life-giving moisture is expressed figurines with gravid breasts, eyes and open mouths from which water flows; zig-zag and m-shaped strokes appear below breasts as a sign of liquidity; double spirals incised over vulvas suggesting rhythmic and tidal flow. Pregnant figurines with delicately bulging abdomens and large belly buttons emphasize the life growing within them. The Goddess's body as vessel was anthropomorphized in nippled ewers and vases with heads for spouts.

Jung connected the life affirming fertility and fruitfulness of the Mother Goddess archetype with certain qualities that show up on the human side: "Maternal solicitude and sympathy, the magic and authority of the female; the wisdom and spiritual exaltation that transcend reason...all that is benign, all that cherishes and sustains, that fosters growth and fertility."[179] Is it any wonder we glorify and essentialize the personal mother in the absence of these archetypal-religious referents in our culture? An awareness of these archetypal patterns offers us a psychological faith—a feeling of transpersonal support—but an absence of this awareness means we often turn people into divinities. As Hillman writes, "Lack of psychological faith is compensated by exaggerated personalizing, a fantastic need for people (and a need for fantastic people)."[180] It is in this light we need to consider the cult of the personal mother and mothering in the culture, wherein mom is either a living saint or the scapegoat for all our emotional and psychological problems. That is, they fail archetypal expectations. "Personifying not allowed as a metaphorical vision returns in concrete form," says Hillman, "we seize upon people, we cling to other persons. They become invested with repressed images so that they grow in importance, become idealized, idolized, while the psyche finds itself more fascinated, more glued and stuck to these concrete individuals than it would have been to the metaphorical persons that are at the root of the projection onto people. Without metaphorical persons, we are forced into desperate clutching literalisms."[181]

FIGURE 9. GODDESS OF LAUSSEL
(LIMESTONE RELIEF, AURIGNACIAN,
SOUTHWESTERN FRANCE, C. 25,000 B.C.)

This elemental depths of mother-knowing is perhaps no more provocatively displayed than by the Goddess of Laussel, a Paleolithic ancestor of Neolithic religion. Carved upon a large overhanging rock within a cavern, the figure is holding a bison horn in her right hand while her left hand rests on her abdomen. Her body overflows from the rock surface as she turns her face toward the horn. The thirteen incisions on the horn are notches that reckon time, specifically the thirteen nights between a new moon and full moon, and from the full to dark moon.[182] The moon is one of the oldest symbols of the cycle of birth, death and rebirth on display each and every month. Turning toward the horn while gesturing to her belly, the Laussel Goddess suggests there is a likeness between her body and the crescent moon-like object. She gazes upon the horn as if saying, *the moon's rhythm is similar to my own*. In other words, the body of the goddess as Nature is like the body of the moon, plural and changeable yet singular and constant. Giving birth, flourishing, dying and being reborn, the mystery of the eternal cycle of life is the mystery of the Great Mother Goddess. This archaic image likewise figures the ancient link between a woman's *menarche* or menstruation cycle and the moon.

The breasts of the Neolithic Great Mother are resplendently full with the milk of life. The anthropomorphic figure (figure 10) with a long neck is part bird and part woman. She holds her left breast as an offering, and in this simple gesture the essence of the archetypal Mother is communicated—she gives of herself. Her left forearm is marked by hatch lines, emphasizing the dynamic energy in the lifting and proffering of her breast. The fullness of the Mother Goddess's body and her generosity stands in sharp relief to that of the Kore as rendered in the archaic Greek sculptural tradition. The Erythrai Kore (figure 11) was discovered in Erythrai's acropolis on the podium of Athena, and though headless, she communicates an active stillness as she steps forward. Her left hand is open and pressed against her breast which swells below from the pressure she applies. With this concealing gesture she conveys her virginal containment—this is not a breast that feeds.

FIGURE 10. BIRD GODDESS
(TERRACOTTA, NEOLITHIC, THESSALY,
C. 5900–5700 B.C.)

FIGURE 11. ERYTHRAI KORE
(MARBLE, ARCHAIC, GREECE,
C. 575–555 B.C.)

This contrast between the archaic Greek Kore and the Neolithic Mother Goddess illustrates a striking observation Erich Neumann made in his study of the Mother archetype. He noticed how the accentuation of the breasts seen in many Mother Goddesses depict the instinctive life urge for physical nourishment and the processes of matter, whereas figures with smaller breasts pointed towards the mysteries of spiritual transformation and the Virgin archetype.[183] That is to say, Kore-Virgin nourishment is spiritual rather than physical, and the small breasts that are a hallmark of all the archaic statues symbolize the deliberate restriction of the kind of nourishment that the Mother provides. The Kore keeps the nourishment and energy that springs forth to herself. These figures clearly render a critical distinction between the Mother and Kore archetypes. The Virgin goddesses of the Greek tradition show how the Kore does not wear her fertility on her sleeve because she does not want to be seeded in the way the Mother Goddess does. Where the Kore is contained and unto-herself, the Mother Goddess is exuberant and sexually fecund, and these qualities extend into the Mother Goddess's Death aspect where her fertility and sexuality are undiminished.

The Great Goddess bears both the Death and Regeneratrix faces in striking measure. Her death-bringing powers are personified by other anthropomorphic figures that combine the female body with birds of prey, particularly the vulture and the owl. In one of the bulls-head shrines in Çatal Huyuk, a Neolithic site in modern-day Turkey, plaster breasts protrude from the wall within which are vulture skulls, positioned so that where the nipple would be is a vulture's beak. Discussing this, Joseph Campbell pertly remarks, "She who feeds, eats back."[184] Jung also addressed this life-taking aspect of the Mother Goddess, who is apt to be connected, he says, to "any devouring and enticing animal."[185] In this dark guise, the Mother Goddess connotes what is "secret, hidden, dark…anything that devours, seduces and poisons, that is terrifying and inescapable like fate."[186] These figures are starkly devouring, a trait we may readily relate to her claim on the imagination. One of the reasons for our tendency to elevate and idealize motherhood is our loss of contact with this aspect of the Mother archetype, which is now only to be found in the debased and symptomatic forms of Dr. Phil exposés and avenging memoirs about devouring mothers. The lost contact with the dark side of this archetype is also implicated in the rarified images of the Virgin Mary, which have dominated the Christian worldview and produced a confusing blend of Kore and Mother.

While death symbolism is prominent in the Neolithic religion, the emphasis appears not to rest in this death-bringing aspect of the Goddess but rather in the oscillating power of renewal and rebirth. A cache of burial urns shaped as owls once carried the bones of the deceased (figure 12). Their large open vulvas, belly buttons with serpentine umbilical cords and breasts indicate they are at the same time vessels of life. These piquant owls illustrate the paradoxical conjunction that is a feature of the uroboric nature of the Mother archetype.

352-364-
1356

FIGURE 12. OWL-SHAPED BURIAL URNS
(CLAY, BRONZE, GREECE, C. 3000–2500 B.C.)

The mythological and archeological investigations of the Neolithic strata of Western civilization provide the symbolic groundwork for understanding the psychological constellation of the Great Mother. Neumann's opus *The Great Mother* provides a profound portrait of this archetype and its central thematic currents. Her fundamental nature is her totality and unity with nature, for she presides over the entire round of life from birth to death. Neumann refers to this as the elementary character of the feminine. He writes,

> As *elementary character* we designate the aspect of the Feminine that as the Great Round, the Great Container, tends to hold fast to everything that springs from it and to surround it like an eternal substance. Everything born of it belongs

to it and remains subject to it; and even if the individual becomes independent, the Archetypal Feminine relativizes this independence into a nonessential variant of her own perpetual being.[187]

The psychic gravitation of the elementary feminine is towards the unconscious, the primordial womb. All life comes from this source and eventually returns to it, so the pull towards non-differentiation (the unconscious) is constellated by this archetype. Gimbutas' elucidation of the various faces of the Neolithic Great Goddess helps us identify how the symbol of the vessel expresses this polarity at work in the Great Mother. She is both nurturer and devourer, she takes life back in order to birth it anew. As the entire cycle of creation, death and renewal is encompassed by the Great Goddess who personifies the primordial nexus of being from which all life and consciousness emerges, both biologically and psychologically. So in regards to the archetype of the feminine, Neumann

places the elementary life giving and life taking character of the Great Mother as primary.

As it turns out, Neumann's treatment of the Great Mother is not the only aspect of his overall vision of the feminine archetype. In his mapping of this complex pattern, he identifies two contrasting axes which he calls "elementary" and "transformative." We have just seen the elementary which is comprised of the light and dark aspects of the Great Mother. Along the transformative axis, Neumann positions that Kore at the positive end and the destructive witch at the negative end. The transformative character follows the elementary but in a distinctive way for it has to do with driving change. Where the elementary is conservative and static, the transformative is mutable and dynamic. This makes movement the primary quality of the transformative feminine, which in its positive manifestation has to do with development of potential; it is future oriented. Whereas its negative manifestation is regressive and constrictive. The emphasis on change that characterizes the transformative aspect is what Neumann identifies as central to the anima or personified soul which, as we know, can also manifest negatively and become a destructive presence in a woman's life. Where the elementary is marked by cyclic processes of continuity, in the positive transformative character independence and individuality are the center of gravity, which we can now locate as belonging in the territory of the Kore-Virgin. Figures like the Muses and Sophia that have to do with what Neumann calls inspiration mysteries belong to this larger pattern, to which in broad terms he locates the archetypes of the Virgin, Muse, and Young Witch. All these figures have to do with initiation into a consciousness that is soulful and spiritual in contrast to biological maturation which is the province of the Mother.

The stasis and conservatism of the elementary juxtaposed by the movement and flow of the transformative are the two aspects that, for Neumann, broadly delineate the feminine energies of the psyche. Together these two lead to the creative matrix of life that belongs to this archetype. Neumann writes,

> If we survey the whole of the symbolic sphere determined by the *vessel* character of the Archetypal Feminine, we find that in its elementary and transformative character the Feminine as 'creative principle' encompasses the whole world. This is the *totality of nature* in its original *unity*, from which all life arises and unfolds, assuming, in its highest transformation, the form of the spirit.[188] [Italics added].

While Neumann makes it clear that the Great Mother belongs to one axis of the archetype of the feminine, she takes on a kind of unitive centrality. His privileging of the Great Mother in this way also has the effect of overshadowing the transformative aspect.

That Neumann begins to see with the Mother-eye makes itself more evident in the way he discusses the transformative character of the feminine via the figures of Persephone and Demeter, who render these two poles of the feminine, personifying the axis of the transformative Virgin and the elementary Mother. Persephone is a Kore-Virgin goddess whose entire mythos is marked by movement and change, while Demeter personifies the unitive and conservative energies of the Mother. However, Neumann eschews the archetypal polarity and winds up not only focusing primarily on the mothering aspects but turning Persephone-Virgin into

Mother. This is most evident in his discussion of the Eleusinian Mysteries where he presents them as what can only be characterized as Mother mysteries. Focusing on Persephone's initiation and return to Demeter as a fulfillment of the Great Mother, he interprets the ritual revelation of the child Brimos (or Iacchus) as Persephone's child, and turns Persephone herself into a Mother.[189] In so doing, he doesn't stick to the mythic image and with the figure of Persphone as she appears, which is as Kore. This is critical, because when Neumann turns the Kore into the Mother in this way, he risks erasing her essential beingness. Persephone loses the spiritual underworld aspect of her nature as well as her identity as a goddess distinct from Demeter.

Persephone as infertile underworld goddess was paramount in the Greek imagination. Classicist Gunther Zuntz asserts, "She is the total negation of life; to think her as a giver of life would be preposterous. Accordingly, her marriage with Aidoneus [Hades] must be without issue; as indeed it is in Homer and all authoritative tradition, the goddess of death is barren."[190] Any interpretation that identifies Persephone with future life in a procreative Mother way does not accord with the essential nature of this figure. While in the Orphic and Eleusinian cult versions of her myth Persephone gives birth to a child, Zuntz argues that these versions do not invalidate the primary identity of Persephone as childless. In this vein, he insightful notes how in Homer, "the orbit of Demeter and Persephone never touch,"[191] which keeps the original sovereignty of Persephone intact as well as conveying the distinctness of their realms and powers. Persephone never becomes a mother, thus she does not have a share in the Mother archetype. As the paradigmatic Kore, Persephone's essence is her virginity.

This Great Mother entrancement is similarly at work in Anne Baring and Jules Cashford's *The Myth of the Goddess*, where all goddesses are Mother Goddesses. Inanna, Ishtar, Isis, Tiamat, Hera, Artemis, Athena and Gaia are seen for their maternal functions, which they believe at some point were subsumed and negated by the patriarchal cultures that appropriated them. The various goddess traditions, they argue, form a unitary image of the Great Mother because of the underlying theme of the primary unity of all life. "We feel entitled to talk of 'the myth of the goddess' since the underlying vision expressed in all the variety of goddess images is constant: the vision of life as a living unity."[192] Unity, in their argument seems to imply a singularity that needs to be represented in both the figures as well as in the idea. They infer in all the mythologies of the various goddesses there is a singular focus on the Mother and child relationship,

> The Mother Goddess, wherever she is found, is an image that inspires and focuses a perception of the universe as an organic, live and sacred whole, in which humanity, the Earth and all life on Earth participate as 'her children.' Everything is woven together in one cosmic web, where all orders of manifest and unmanifest life are related, because all share in the sanctity of the original source.[193]

Here we see the way the Great Mother archetype saturates our understanding of the Goddess, encompassing all feminine figures into her own form. This tendency towards Mother Goddess domination is an issue David Kinsley has discussed in the field of religious studies, "Too often it is assumed or implied that if a deity is female, her sex dominates her character. It is assumed or implied that she is associated with motherhood, fertility, and the earth for example…However, the diversity of characteristics and roles played by goddesses goes far beyond such simplification. Some goddesses have nothing to do with motherhood, fertility, or the earth."[194] Clearly the issue of seeing by means of the Mother-eye is not a problem that only assails depth psychologists.

Gimbutas' archeomythological excavations of the Neolithic civilization provide ancient threads of the Great Mother goddess, its primary worldview and symbolic expressions. Partnering her research with Neumann's study of the symbolism of the Great Mother archetype clearly renders the psychological ideas and currents of this pattern of consciousness. A great variety is presented in the material by all four scholars: Gimbutas' Neolithic goddesses express the three distinct realms of birth, death and renewal, Neumann's elementary Mother is partnered by the transformative Virgin, and Baring and Cashford's study span hundreds of female divinities from many mythologies. It is striking that despite the variety of goddesses, their distinct powers and archetypal patterns these studies make visible, it is the Great Mother who is enthroned not only as primary, which she certainly is, but who is then taken to be the central essence of all goddesses. Gimbutas is clear in her understanding that it is a single Great Mother who has many faces, a view shared by Baring and Cashford. And for Neumann, all mythological female figures become symbols of the Great Mother. The result is that they return every figure to its source—the Great Mother. In so doing, they not only exhibit the archetypal force characteristic of this pattern of consciousness, namely the psychic gravitational pull toward non-differentiation as a return to her, they simultaneously demonstrate the loss of differentiation and particularity that are the hallmarks of Kore consciousness.

That the Mother Goddess is the oldest divinity perceived by humankind is attested by the Paleolithic documents of civilization that range from snow cloaked Siberia to sun drenched Spain. The primacy of the Great Mother Goddess in the history of human consciousness, both personally and collectively, is not under contention. What is under scrutiny is the way the Mother works in our vision. If there is a problem with the quality of vision that the Mother archetype conditions it is how everything is returned back to her, back to the vessel, where a more undifferentiated consciousness resides. When we are seeing by means of the Great Mother, all goddesses are ultimately one, and are all mothers. In this way, these works illustrate exactly how an archetype, as Neumann admits, is a "pattern of vision" that exerts an influence "on consciousness and the specific direction of the mind."[195] These authors were not just writing about the archaeological, mythological and symbolic evidence of this archetype, they were also writing under the influence of the archetype. Perhaps this is the nature of these studies. I have no doubt that I also write driven by the Kore's own need to break into our contemporary awareness.

In some fields that aspire to scientific objectivity, this might seem a hindrance or even a distortion, but in fields touched by depth psychological and comparative symbolism, there's an acknowledgement that our perspectives partake of the patterns of knowing that are at the same time the topics of our study. Jung once wrote, "there is no Archimedean point from which to judge, since the psyche is indistinguishable from its manifestation. The psyche is the object of psychology, and—fatally enough—its subject at the same time and there is no getting away from this fact."[196] Hillman too notes the dominance of the Mother in Neumann's work and exhibits this point about his hermeneutics: "Of course one finds the 'Great Mother' every where if the 'Great Mother' is the archetype dominating the searchers vision."[197] The point is not to eschew this psychological factor but to try to see it at work.

In sum, the Great Mother is a vesseling and containing condition of consciousness whereby individuality is returned to primordial oneness. The Mother as an archetypal lens of perception is at work when, for example, in discussing feminine divinities we use the singular phrase "the goddess," or see all goddesses as Mother goddesses. The containing and unitive values of the Mother archetype are announced by this emphasis on the fundamental *One*. This extends to modes of interpretation or perceptual habits, for as Neumann himself notes, "everything that issues from the darkness within its vessel is looked upon as its offspring and child, and the domination of the Archetypal Feminine over all this constellates the unity and fateful power of the matriarchal world."[198] The Great Mother turns all goddesses into mothers and every other being into her children. Males are all sons and lovers, either battling against her for liberation from the womb or in her service; all females are daughters and avatars of her younger self.

Such understanding aids our handling of the Mother archetype, and her influence on our views become easier to grasp. In approaching the Kore, consciousness of the Mother's great embrace is even more crucial. Nurturing and devouring, the Great Mother obscures the presence of the Kore because autonomy and difference stand in opposition to her principles. The values that belong to the Great Mother including elemental fusion, the return to source, and dissolution of differences, can be imagined simply as expressions of her vesseling nature which takes back all she has given birth to. But the vessel of life can also be the vessel of death, with a regressive, devouring arc that occludes the energy of independence. Writing about the Mother Goddess from a Kore perspective leads to looking at these unitive and encompassing values differently, and perhaps with some suspicion, because the Kore values distinction and individuality. Consciousness requires separation, and Kore sovereignty means standing apart.

CHAPTER SEVEN

Supreme Competence

As an archetypal power that encompasses the instinctual depths of life and the mysteries of nature, the Great Mother is a large and at times overwhelming topic. This is the case especially in terms of women's psychology where the Mother is omnipresent in relation to having a mother, being a mother, and occupying an idealized role expected in explicit and implicit ways. The warp and woof of the Mother is complex and woven into nearly all quarters of life. Here I offer a vignette of where in contemporary American culture our relation to the Great Mother subtly works to preclude Kore consciousness. Exploring a phenomenon that renders sharply the contrasting world-views of the Kore and Mother will help us become more aware of what cultivating the Kore looks like.

Riding under the banner of the Goddess, second wave feminists went into battle for equal opportunities in every sector of life including economics, politics, education, profession, and healthcare. Doors that had been historically closed to women—to colleges, libraries, offices, corner offices, doctors, banks, and voting stations—were opened, clearing a passage beyond the narrow stereotypical gender roles within which women were caught. Their battle cry: *we can do anything—we'll show them, we can have it all.* Out of that rallying call comes the idea of 'having it all,' what became the shorthand slogan for a woman's balancing of career, love, children, family, friends, and self. The origins of this term can be traced back to the early 1980s in what Jennifer Szalai describes as a corporate sell of Helen Gurley Brown's book "Having it All," which outlined what she called the Mouseburger Plan.[199] This plan detailed how the average woman with no particular gifts, but who is willing to work hard, can create the full life she wants. Based on Gurley Brown's own experience of growing up with nothing in a rural area and becoming the editor of Cosmopolitan Magazine in New York City, the book was to be a manual for helping women get more out of life. Her publishers gave it its infamous title despite Gurley Brown's fierce objections, and the phrase entered the cultural stream, hitching a ride on second wave feminism.

The ambition to have it all has been inherited by younger generations of women for whom it has been a tacit expectation, but in the midst of the pursuit are encountering unexpected roadblocks. One of these is a struggle differentiating between sociocultural and personal limitations. In Lia Macko and Kerry Rubin's study of women of Generation Y (born between 1977-94), one of the primary issues identified is how because this generation did not have to fight for the rights that earlier feminists established, as recipients of those accomplishments they have difficulty identifying the challenges that continue to be inherent to various socio-cultural structures. Without the battle energy of the second generation feminists, there is not the same sharp critique. Unable to clearly identify the forces at work in the collective sphere, they are prone to personalize the gender inequality issues that lie just beneath the surface, mistaking objective difficulties for personal failures. The resulting introjection of these larger problems inevitably leads to psychological crises.[200] It is as if the Goddess has returned for this younger generation but in an undifferentiated way. The collision between the fantasy of a successful work-life equilibrium and its impossibility due to the socioeconomic realities creates a depth of suffering, and for most people there is no way to bridge the gap without coming undone or getting ill.

The over-exuberance of 'having it all' lost contact with the history of women's struggles for equality and opportunity. Something went astray with the over-identification with this ideal and over-expansive idea of life as a woman. The ambition this catchphrase connotes is not merely the desire to have what men have, it is an undifferentiated reaction to the archetypal feminine that defaults to images of the Great Mother. Even if we can consciously recognize the fallacy due to the socioeconomic, gender and racial forces that make the fulfillment of work-life balance very difficult, there is still an unconscious attempt to fulfill the vision. This appears in the drive for abundance and the expectation of supreme competence in all areas of activity, and because it does not value the inherent limitations of life, it is soul-crushing. Maybe 'having it all' was a flawed idea in the beginning.

The pressure for competence accentuates a wide ranging adeptness to hold each and every possibility on offer. This sensibility is starkly rendered by Ariel Levy in her 2018 memoir *The Rules Do Not Apply*. Levy, a bisexual woman born in the 1970s, felt herself the beneficiary of the women's movement. For her this meant, "I got to have all these choices, and the rules—biological, historical—did not apply…I thought I had harnessed the power of my own strength and greed and love in a life that could contain it."[201] What Levy describes is not only about the difficulties of being a mother and a career woman, it extends to all women in our culture. This vision of mastery is an unconscious attitude that assails women in subtle and overt ways, and is evident in the struggles women express about a basic sense of fulfillment in their lives. Because life vision involves an unconscious identification with the Great Mother, it diminishes the spirit of ordinary human women.

A further complication is that the Great Mother, says Hillman, pertains to that habit of mind that makes all psychological events material ones, "placing the images of the soul in the service of physical tangibilities."[202] It is the earth aspect of the Great Mother that desires the concretization of ideas, because earth as an archetypal element draws us into making things matter. In psychological terms, the need to be supremely competent in all worldly things can be an unconscious attempt to enact the Mother Goddess's creativity. As an archetype, the Mother has a limitless supply of nurturance and energy, but human beings cannot fully realize archetypal patterns. In the attempt to do so we lose touch with ourselves as ordinary persons. We see the woman with a career, kids and marriage frantically racing around trying to attend to each sector and losing contact with her deeper self and ordinary life between it all. It's a kind of ideal abundance in the sense of attempting to have all areas continually blossom, grow, and develop. Without downtime in which being affects doing, without the reflection and pause wherein the invisible vitalities are tended, the soul runs dry. Driven by externals in the attempt to do or have more, we lose our inner integrity.

The fantasy of perpetual giving and availability draws us toward a particularly American problem—giving little if any value to slowing down and reflecting. People don't know how to meaningfully weave a sense of limitation into their lives. Excess rules in this consumerist culture, which is visible not only in the accrual of objects but in the need for constant connection and consumption of media. This excess makes for an easy conjoining to the twin issues of abundance and competency, which 'having it all' echoes. While many now reject this phrase, hearing in it a false promise cooked up in a Madison Avenue publishing house and pinned to the feminist movement, the psychological force that animates it is still afoot. In one way or another it has been assimilated by women whether or not they are, or hope to be, both mothers and professionals. It is also a frame of mind that can't shake off its ties to the American dream of ever-expanding success.

The desire for all facets of experience to be available simultaneously is another way the appetite for more can appear. After a miscarriage and losing her wife to alcoholism, Levy realized how much she, and other women in her life, want everything at once: "We want to be youthful adventurers and middle-aged mothers. We want intimacy and autonomy, safety and stimulation, reassurance and novelty, coziness and thrills. But we can't have it all."[203] While Levy's expectations are extreme, she is touching on something true about the simultaneous hunger for the comfort of the bounty as well as the prospect of the harvest. The Great Mother is recognizable in this generally unconscious expectation of life that demands equal and ever-increasing plenty.

The problem is not the archetype per se but rather the way in which people unconsciously identify with the archetype, cutting off other modes of being. What's often missing is the value of particularity and the celebration of the limited. The abundance and limitlessness of the Great Mother in this way stands in contrast to the focus and choice of the Kore. The Kore makes sacrifice, differentiates and incubates the unique. The Korai triad goddesses display this in their fields of power—the Fates whose hands give form and limitation to our lives, and the Hours who keep measure of the right order and rhythms of nature. In terms of orchestrating the parts of feminine being, it is specifically the Kore who mitigates the excesses of the Mother archetype.

The Kore helps women focus and make choices without feeling they are betraying something of their own nature. This brings us back to Esther Harding's powerful articulation of how a woman who is psycho-logically virgin makes choices based on what is true rather than what is pleasing—either to herself or others. This is where Kore sovereignty is its most potent, for her sense of self is not dependent on the approval of others, for she does not recognize any authority as greater than her own. This unto-oneself containment is the precondition for discerning what is necessary, regardless of whether it is understandable or satisfying to anyone else. Choosing to live from the ground of one's reality means that a woman "may have to say no, when it would be easier, as well as more adapted, conventionally speaking, to say yes," writes Harding.[204] Whether the expectations are pressures coming from the wider culture or family, the strength to choose what is right, which can mean saying no, comes from the ground beneath her feet, like that of the archaic Kore.

The women across the globe and over the centuries who rejected the cultural structures that worked to exclude them did so because they were drawing upon an inner integrity of vision. Hildegard of Bingen (1098-1179), the German Benedictine Abbess who was a mystic, philoso-pher, writer and composer, Artemisia Gentileschi (1593-1656) the Italian painter who was the first woman to join the Academy of Art in Florence, and Sojourner Truth (1797-1883) the African-American abolitionist and women's rights activist, all exemplify the courageous spirit that occurs under the influence of the Kore.

This kind of Kore knowing can also be heard in activist Gloria Steinem's reflection about her choice regarding children, "I'm not sure I would have been strong enough to have children, to live that life, and come out the other end with an identity of my own. The way I came to think of it was that I could not give birth to both myself and someone else. It was a choice."[205] While the Mother says, *I want to give all* and therefore support the drive for abundance, the Kore looks for what is authentically hers to have. It's the difference between an undifferentiated fertility that goes with the Great Mother and the particular creativity that goes with the Kore. The difference is that a true creativity needs limits and containment. So it may be the undifferentiated fertility that is behind these fantasies of supreme success. Women want to be fertile, they want to add to life and contribute something to the world, but it must be true to the lineaments of their being in order for there to be a sense of deep fulfillment. Rather than having it all, the Kore seeks to be aligned with what she knows, deep down, already belongs to her. The Kore is what has us cultivate what we value, and it may be a small or large vision, but it is something wrought of our own particular essence. This is germane to the possibility of living a more authentic life.

The Barrier of Cultural Extraversion

We live in a period of Western culture where there is an extraordinary emphasis on external achievement. Girls and women are encouraged to be and do anything, to accomplish their goals, prove their abilities, break the glass ceiling, and change the rules of the game. While change and progress of the culture is necessary, all this activity is turned outward, emphasizing what we do and how it is seen to be activating change out in the world. This constant extraversion is a barrier to inviting contact with the Kore, for as the contained one, it is she who initiates us into an inner sense of self. Women need to be initiated into the Kore's introversion so to attain some vision of inner values, which ensures our outer activities are in alignment with our deeper nature.

Feminism has opened the door to the Kore by revealing our unconscious adoption of patriarchal values, for example, the default ways women have been objectified and denied the same rights as men. But there is a more unconscious way of falling into patriarchy, which is to abandon one's inner life for outer activity. This is not to suggest women forego the cultural sphere, but it does pertain to the way one participates. The patriarchal outlook has been quite successful coopting and codifying the roles of Mother and Daughter. The archetypal Daughter relates to the family (personal and collective) through service, and the Mother gives much nourishment. In the patriarchal paradigm, both roles are essentially selfless, which has given rise to the phenomenon of women having no archetypal anchor that would secure an identity based on independence. Because of this absent ballast, it seems that women then unconsciously succumb to the patriarchal game and align with its values which emphasize external success through competitiveness, hierarchal power dynamics and dominance. As poet and feminist scholar Adrienne Rich articulated, "No woman is really an insider in the institutions fathered by masculine consciousness. When we allow ourselves to believe we are, we lose touch with parts of ourselves defined as unacceptable by that consciousness."[206] When women try to play the game structured by those values, they are forced to give up or sacrifice part of their soul.

Coming into relationship with the Kore means withdrawing from collectivized values as primary arbiters of one's own, and instead locating truth in the sanctum of one's inner life. By contrast, anyone whose psychological attitude towards life is defined by dependency on something or someone outside herself, whether it is another person, social opinion or collective principle, is not in touch with the Kore. As the untouchable Virgin, the Kore is not bound through external relationship. Because of this radical shift in psychic direction, initiation into the reality of the Kore is understandably difficult for both women and men. Animated by what Jung called "the spirit of the times," our culture demands an outward orientation to life and participation in the collective signifiers that run counter to the individual in search of their inner ground. However, a sense of self is ultimately wrought from within, in connection to the psyche and the values that are fashioned by the soul of each person.

What standing in the world from the Kore ground of one's being feels like is strikingly illustrated in novelist Muriel Barbery's description of a Maori football player performing the *haka* aboriginal warrior dance.

While this athlete is a man going into battle, as a style of consciousness the Kore's particular quality of contained presence can be discerned in women and men alike. The quality of presence Barbery describes is attributable to the connection one has to their core and the potency that comes from that connection. This particular athlete captivated the eyes of everyone in the crowd because, "while the others' gestures went toward their adversaries and the entire stadium who were watching, this player's gestures stayed inside him, stayed focused upon him, and that gave him an unbelievable presence and intensity. And so the haka, which is a warrior chant, gained all its strength from him…That Maori player was like a tree, a great indestructible oak with deep roots and a powerful radiance—everyone could feel it. And yet you also got the impression that the great oak could fly, that it would be as quick as the wind, despite, or perhaps because of, its deep roots."[207] This strength comes from concentration on being present to one's inner fire rather than outer impact. His presence is imbued with an intensity that is both deep and light, a kind of motionless motion that is rooted and at the same time can soar.

Integrity to one's own call comes from within and also means outer constraint, a hallmark of Kore consciousness. In contrast, heroic cultural extroversion sees determination and ambition as the function women must own and hone in order to succeed, neglectful of the way all human life comes with limitations—inner and outer, concrete and psychological, familial and cultural, historical and economic. A belief in one's self-made agency cannot forever mask a sense of one's truth and essential nature born of this existential sobriety, which gives life character and meaning. Alignment with the guiding principles of the soul means challenging our personal ego desires and locating ultimate authority in the domain of a transpersonal power or god figure. While we cannot author or control everything that happens, we can love and partner the specific shape of our lives, barriers and limitations included. *Amor fati*, the love of one's fate, is one of the Kore's favored prayers and a sense of fate has everything to do with connecting to a sense of purpose.

There's also something about our connection with the Kore that helps keep women from over-identifying with other archetypal principles. This is because the Kore brings us back to the vital truths of our feeling. Being able to discern how we feel means being able to sort between what is ours and what's playing a role. Another way to imagine into this is that Kore containment helps us know when we're deviating from our personal limits. Identifying with any archetype means attempting to transcend human limits, but this is heightened by the Mother archetype's unbounded life nurturing aspect. For example, an over identification with the Great Mother could be the difference between creating a safe nurturing place for our loved ones and attempting to be that safe nurturing place. The woman who has come into relationship with the Kore is someone with the ability to mother with boundaries, which can appear as an investment in the individuality of the child, so that they are also, in the end, fed from within by their own nature.

In order for us to become psychologically healthier, the human mother, Jung suggests, must be relieved from carrying the burden of the archetypal pattern.[208] We must consider this in terms of what we project onto our personal mother, but, as I have attempted to draw out, we must also look at where this is at work in women's unrealistic expectations of themselves. A common example of over identification with the Great Mother is in the way women's primary sense of self value comes to reside in their ability to have children. When this is the case, the emotional and psychological costs can be very painful. Nini Herman writes how, "a moment of profound depression, which we today call menopausal, will darken a woman's life as long as she equates creativity with fertility, rather than envisaging her new spheres of influence. For these may well turn out to be quite rich and rewarding provided that limits are accepted, and that which *is* is not attacked if it is not everything."[209] This sense of limitation as well as the creative challenges of exploring oneself at different stages of life, which are intrinsic to the Kore, acts as a kind of antidote to the abundant growth the Great Mother prizes. It is the health of women across the spectrum of life that hangs in the balance with this work of not identifying with the archetype.

All this leads us to acknowledge that there is a crisis around mothering. The unitive value found at the core of the Great Mother dominates our unconscious relationship with her, particularly in the absence of more awareness of all the different sides of this archetypal figure. In a culture bereft of differentiated feminine sensibilities, we miss the complexity her three Neolithic faces illustrate, as discussed in the last chapter. This complexity is especially lost when we split off the dark side of the Mother configuration. Of course, this darkness can leap out and attach itself to any instance of 'failed' mothering wherein anything short of perfection is equated with failure. This all or nothing expectation stands in contrast to what psychoanalyst Donald Winnicott called the "good enough mother," which describes the mother who is conscious of her limitations and can successfully ease her children into that awareness.

That we live in a time of disruptive change in the myths women have been living is powerfully illustrated in Peggy Orenstein's book *Flux: Women on Sex, Work, Love, Kids, and Life in a Half-Changed World*. Interviewing hundreds of women in their twenties, thirties and forties to elucidate the issues of career, marriage, and motherhood, she recounts how the discussions ran the gamut in terms of their expectations, hopes and the realities. From the youthful idealism of the twenties, to the realities in their thirties and the opening vistas of their forties, Orenstein felt that she had come to learn a few things about women in this time of flux including: the vital connection between a woman's sexual agency and her sense of self; equal partnership marriages as central to leading fuller lives; relinquishing the Good Mother and its unattainable standards; having a plan for one's life that includes being on one's own.[210] All these pieces point toward the same constellation, that a woman's sense of self, finding her voice, and knowing some autonomy, are all essential to feeling fulfillment in one's life. That agency, sovereignty, and consciousness of one's feelings and needs are becoming central makes the archetypal pattern clear—the quality of a woman's life depends on the quality of her relationship to the Kore.

CHAPTER EIGHT

Return to Demeter & Persephone:
the Mother, Daughter and Kore

The Great Mother casts a powerful spell. Yet, as we have seen, examining this spell makes visible the Kore who personifies qualities of being that the Mother pattern obscures. Another contributing factor in this regard has been the conflation of the Daughter and Kore archetypes. This is partly due to the Great Mother wanting to see everyone as her children. No myth offers such rich insights into this special problem like that of Demeter and Perse-phone. We therefore return to this myth in order to re-vision it and draw new insights that further the articulation of Kore consciousness and values. As one of the aims of this study is to recover the Kore dimension that has been overshadowed by other goddess figures, my treatment of Persephone differs from that of other depth psychological writers.[211]

While Persephone is the prime exemplar of the Kore, she has generally been discussed as the archetypal Daughter whose identity is primarily dependent on Demeter. This situation is revealed by many book indexes wherein individual entries for Persephone or Kore are simply followed by "See Demeter and Persephone." Claire Douglas's *The Woman in the Mirror,* which provides an authoritative and exhaustive review of Jungian literature on feminine psychology, has but one entry under Persephone followed by "see Demeter," and no entry for Kore. This provides us with a snapshot of how this goddess has been treated. Just as Hillman helped us recognize the Hero and the Son are distinct archetypal figures that are often overlapped, so too the Kore and Daughter.[212]

Obviously in the figure of Persephone we have both Kore and Daughter. But the way in which each element is underscored and treated in our reflections is what is in need of closer examination. In broad terms, the Daughter is defined by her relationship to parental powers whose authority provide the defining contours, positive or negative, of her world. Being protected is one primary characteristic of the Daughter, as well as the motif of belonging to Mother or Father. Persephone gathering flowers in the field is often referred to as "Demeter's Kore" and "The Kore that belongs to Demeter." Athena is a Daughter of the Father, as she is born from her father's head and claims being for the Father always and above all. "No mother gave me birth. I honor the male, in all things but marriage. Yes, with all my heart I am my Father's child," she states in Aeschylus' *The Eumenides*.[213] Both these goddesses illustrate the particular idea of ownership that is a part of the Daughter archetype.

In contrast to this quality of possession that constellates with the Daughter, the Kore recognizes no authority above her own because she is sovereign; the contours of her being are drawn from within herself. The etymological trail assists in distinguishing the territory of the Kore from the Daughter—the Greek *kore* is neither equivalent to, nor shares roots with, the word for daughter, *thygater*, the Proto-Indo-European root of which means "the (potential) suckler, the one that draws milk."[214] The Daughter draws her sustenance from the parental breast, whereas the Kore, whose root means life force, emerges with a vitality from her own seed essence. Detached from Mother and Father, the Kore is not defined by her past, or the family and its inheritances. Something else makes her distinct, which is the sense that she begins and ends with herself. Thus, at the beginning of the myth we must conclude that Persephone is not yet Kore despite that being her name. It is only in the course of the entire myth that Persephone comes into the fullness of the Kore archetype.

Both Daughter and Kore patterns are visible in Athena, as she is born a Virgin goddess dressed in armor, and decries belonging to Father Zeus.

While Persephone also displays a Daughter aspect, it is neither primary or perpetual. This is crucial. It is the Mother-eye that reads the myth and this goddess in this light. We may remember that Persephone moves between being with her mother in the upper world and being with Hades in the underworld, ruling as its queen. In her person, Persephone combines Daughter and Kore along with Queen, the latter two underscoring the primacy of her autonomy and power. The ancient sovereignty of Persephone is evidenced in her worship in Sicily where she was a pre-Greek underworld divinity who only later became linked to Demeter.[215] However, because the principal version of Persephone's myth comes to us in the *Homeric Hymn to Demeter* composed in honor of the mother goddess, Persephone's sovereignty is not as easily seen.

Myths are read as ways of illuminating human problems in the search for psychological understanding. In this vein, the myth of Demeter and Persephone has been predominantly read in two ways—first, in terms of the mother and daughter relationship, and second, in how both ancient Western matrifocal culture, women and feminine consciousness has been brutalized by patriarchal values. These two approaches to the Persephone myth often focus on the underlying primacy of the mother-daughter bond, and the emphasis on their reunion which reinstates the original connection before its rupture by Zeus and Hades who personify the patriarchal forces that conspired to separate Persephone from Demeter. Kathie Carlson's *Life's Daughter/Death's Bride* exemplifies this interpretation, emphasizing Persephone's abduction as a negative and violent breach, Persephone's resistance to Hades, as well as her eagerness to return to her mother. Seeing the myth as dramatizing the antagonistic powers of patriarchy and matriarchy, Carlson's work tackles an admittedly important sociocultural problem and its psychological implications for mother-daughter relationships. Underscoring the divisive influence of patriarchal culture in the mother-daughter bond, she argues psychological separation is not necessary in women's relational development, deeming the emphasis on separation as a condition for consciousness and individuation which reflects the "masculine conditioning in our culture."[216] This vision of relational fusion which Carlson advocates as the natural and proper ground for women's psychological development belongs to the archetypal field of the Mother, for whom separation is antithetical to the values of containment and non-differentiation.

Reading the myth from Persephone's point of view, we see how initiation into Kore consciousness occurs through the rupture of the primal mother-daughter union. As the main motif in the myth is separation, this is actually the primary concern of the archetypal Mother-Daughter dyad. Implicit to this theme of severance is a woman's coming into her authenticity, what Herman calls "possession of her unencumbered truth," and requires working with one of the deepest and essential problems in the mother-daughter relationship, which is the "subversion of authenticity."[217] This interpersonal psychological survival tactic occurs when approval is sought by acting in accord with what one's mother desires, hiding who we are in order to play a role. In the Homeric Hymn, when Persephone returns from Hades she says to Demeter she was forced to eat the pomegranate seeds that now binds her to him. But is that really what happened or is that Daughter trying to calm Mother down? In Persephone's account, there is an eager emphasis on her unknowing innocence that we cannot fail to pick up on. Sensing what her mother wants of her, the daughter hides who she has become in order to appease. Staying related to one's mother can sometimes feel just as essential as being oneself, and the collision of these fundamental needs can present a tremendous psychological challenge. The roots of this dynamic are based on an archetypal triangulation of the Great Mother, Daughter and Kore. Authenticity comes from the Greek *authentes* "one acting on one's own authority," and from *autos* "self" from which we get author. This Kore impulse for authorship and authenticity is subverted when the creative tension between these inner figures becomes a collusion of the Daughter with the Mother. In hiding her identity to stay within the relational bonds as defined by the Mother, the Kore is silenced in the woman. It is in this vein that I understand Herman's point that "until our awareness of the many-fold subversions to woman's authenticity within the mother-daughter dyad becomes more robust and astute, womanness remains subject to perennial regression."[218]

Herman's radical insight on this complex dynamic helps us recognize how separation from the Mother acts as a threshold between the fields of consciousness personified by the Daughter and Kore. From this vantage point, Persephone's abduction from her Mother by Hades is an archetypal necessity; it is what allows her korehood to come into full articulation. But before we turn more fully to the conditions of this blossoming, we must look at the difficulties that the Mother encounters in this process. The Homeric Hymn tells of Demeter's anguish when her daughter disappears and her rage at Zeus for having given her daughter away, which leads the Mother of the Grain to show her dark death face.

> [She] made this the most terrible year on this earth that feeds so many, and the most cruel. The earth did not take seed that year, for Demeter in her beautiful crown concealed it. And the cattle many times pulled their bent ploughs in vain over the land, and many times the white barley fell uselessly upon the earth. And in fact she would have wiped out the whole race of talking men with a painful famine, and deprived those who live on Olympus of the glorious honor of offerings and sacrifices, if Zeus hadn't noticed it, and had thought about it in his heart.[219]

When the Mother suffers, everyone suffers.

Herman observes how the loss of her daughter brings Demeter into a violent confrontation with time. Eternally fertile, the archetypal Mother is not herself bound by the limits of existence, so the loss of her daughter wounds Demeter's desire (and nature) to be creative forever. The other facet that is part of the Mother-Daughter pattern at work in Demeter's psychology is identification. Demeter is not quite able to see her daughter as separate from her, which is suggestively implied in the Hymn by the way Persephone is at times referred to as Demeter's slim-ankled daughter rather than by her own name. This part of Demeter's fury is due to how it is beyond her understanding that she and Persephone should be separated, she expects always to have her daughter beside her. In these ways the values of the Mother come into sharp conflict with the emerging Kore and the masculine energies that are constellated around her. Overwhelmed by this loss and the undermining of her power, Demeter, Herman says, "suffers a near disintegration,"[220] which speaks to the deep psychological ties that bind mothers to daughters.

This archaic conflict between Mother and Kore is what Erich Neumann described as the dynamic between the elementary and transformative feminine energies of the psyche, discussed in chapter six. The transformative character disrupts the established order that is the territory of the elementary feminine as personified by the Great Mother, who holds and contains.[221] Persephone personifies the transformative aspect of the feminine energy, which when released from the Mother's embrace, steps forward into new life, ushering in new values and perspectives.

While this myth confronts us with many dark and difficult features—Persephone's rape and abduction, Demeter's anguish and depression due to their separation—we must recognize that Persephone's identity comes from these very things. By virtue of the fissure, the Kore is released, born from the space between Daughter and Mother. The Kore finds her poise and her connection to the spirit of being by embracing those events announcing her destiny. This is the way I understand how in the Hymn, Persephone's name appears for the first time when Hermes descends to the underworld to speak with her and Hades. Bringing with him a message from Zeus that says she must return to the upper world so that Demeter's famine can come to an end, Hermes calls her "holy and pure (*hagne*) Persephone."[222] Persephone's holy purity is her Kore nature, which is inviolable. This scene suggests that her underworld descent makes possible the advent of her name for it is here at last that she inhabits herself fully. The paradox is that the recognition of her korehood occurs after being raped and abducted. This impresses the metaphorical versus sociological reading upon us—her underworld initiation leads to her sovereignty. Without the rupture of the primal Mother-Daughter bond Persephone would remain a nameless daughter forever in the folds of her mother's gown.

It is the role of the animus to break open the Mother-Daughter dyad and usher in Kore consciousness. As Marion Woodman points out, this myth illuminates how psychologically it is the arrival of, and subsequent surrender to, the masculine principle that allows separation from the mother to occur.[223] The spiritedness that Zeus, Hades and Hermes per-

Masculine energies

sonify fertilizes movement, disturbing the soporific hold Demeter-Mother has maintained. This is the masculine aspect of a woman's psyche that engenders differentiation, focus, and the discernment of values which serve the creative impulse toward individuality. The arrival of these masculine energies signal the arrival of a previously unknown creativity, what Woodman identifies as making possible not only the development of a woman's individual beingness, but also a renewal: "In the individual woman's life, in a natural life cycle, the old value system (Demeter) grieves, while the new value system (Persephone) is ravished by the otherness that penetrates her and brings new life; then old and new are reunited in a new way."[224] From this perspective we can look to Hades and see how his actions more fully establish Persephone's sovereignty—he abducts her out from under Demeter's shadow and ensures she cannot return by giving her the pomegranate.

Acting as an agent in her unfolding, Hades activates Persephone's initiation into korehood. Psychologically, we could say that for the Kore, those painful experiences of separation from parental imagos, their authority and the protective naivety the parental field often attempts to prolong, are in service to her emerging individuality. The greater the psychological fusion of the daughter with her mother, the greater the force of their separation. "Where the woman is caught in unconscious identification with the mother," writes Woodman, "then she has to be raped out of the identification before she can find her own individuality."[225] This sounds harsh, even offensive, but we're not describing any literal action here, only an inner movement mythically rendered. The goddesses and gods of myth are not human persons, nor do they describe our life actions. They are metaphors of the inner life of the psyche.

Differentiated korehood demands a transformation of consciousness or a change of attitude. As Hillman says, we are all Persephone who need to find our way out of Mother's clutches.[226] However, our resistance to this is revealed in the way we want to think Persephone should never have been abducted and taken away from Demeter. From this perspective, says Herman, "Mother should have her daughter back, at home with her, where she belongs. This feeling only underwrites how powerfully a part of us remains rooted in the past that each traveled through in infancy, where there was no room for father in that dyadic embrace: where the Elementary Feminine Character, holding and not letting go, maintained its unchallenged rule."[227]

The task of separating from the parental forces is paramount to living our authenticity. Again, the masculine spirit is a crucial part of this process as illustrated by the small but pivotal role Helios, the Sun, plays in the drama. When Demeter learns of Zeus's role in her daughter's disappearance, she turns her anger on him. In response to her rage at Zeus, Helios remarks, "is not Hades a worthy match for your daughter?" As solar consciousness clarifies form, so Helios names the emerging reality that is at complete odds with Demeter's reality. To connect with this solar essence is "to reach the place where we belong to ourselves," which Woodman and Dickinson say requires our having, "to sever the umbilical cord that binds us to archaic dependencies."[228]

In the Hymn, it is only after her descent and marriage that Persephone is recognized as a goddess in her own right. While she is fated to spend her year separated into thirds, one part with Hades in the underworld, and two parts in the upper world with her mother and the other gods, it is all contained in the fullness of her sovereign korehood. That is to say, the Kore is the one who embraces her fate. In so doing, Demeter is forced to recognize Persephone's agency, for she moves through the worlds in her own time and in a rhythm that is hers alone.

Persephone and Demeter locate in mythic time the special relationship and challenges of the archetypal Mother and Kore. The myth also shows us where the mother-daughter break and subsequent consciousness in this dyad begins. We could therefore say this is an origin story of the birth of consciousness out of the matrix of the Mother. While this myth helps us imagine into the archetypal relationship of the Kore and the Mother, it is only by the Kore eventually finding her way out of her mother's embrace that their distinction can become a syncopation. Even if their reunion into a new and more fulfilling conjunction is our ultimate aim, as the alchemists knew, "only separated things can unite."[229] Mother and Kore in a woman's psyche can only effect a symbolic psychological conjunction if there is differentiation of the Daughter from the Kore, and separation of the primal Mother-Daughter fusion. Persephone's becoming shines a light on the processes by which a woman who is psychologically Daughter becomes psychologically Kore.

The Kore aspect of a woman's psyche does not fear or resent the rending of the Mother-Daughter dyad. This is something that the myth of Medusa and Athena can help us to understand, though it requires that we approach this story from an entirely different angle wherein Medusa personifies the Mother and Athena the Daughter become Kore. Medusa's gaze turns all she beholds to stone, and both Herman and Woodman see this as the dark face of the Great Mother, specifically the Terrible Mother who paralyzes those who try to leave her, whether as an absconder or interloper. In psychological terms, the extreme form of the Medusa complex, Woodman writes, "does petrify in that it stops the flow of life, the natural giving and receiving of energy."[230] The dark Mother is the one who denies movement and change.

After Perseus kills Medusa, Athena affixes her head to her breastplate. On this mysterious act, Herman asks, "Was it not for Athene that the hero had set out to conquer the appalling monster?...Must every Kore not stand in relentless opposition to this entangling aspect of the mother who would wind her coils about her and never let her go?"[231] Athene with Medusa on her breast is the Kore who is neither overwhelmed by the Mother nor dissociated from her. This is the "radical shift from identification with the mother to standing in her own shoes on her own ground,"[232] that Woodman sees at the heart of a woman coming into her beingness. This is imagined as Athena-Kore bearing the dark Mother upon her chest in full recognition. Again we see how differentiation is made possible through the assistance of the masculine energy of the psyche, here the figure of Perseus. To the undifferentiated mother-daughter dyad, masculinity appears a brutal disruptor, but this same masculinity becomes an integral part of the initiated Kore. This integral masculine spirit, or animus, is suggested by the erect phallic form of the archaic Kore statues. The graceful containment of their upright posture and the active forward step is a display of this extraordinary inner union of masculine and feminine energy.

None of the foregoing is to suggest the Mother is no longer an important psychic pattern for women. For Jung, the myth of Demeter and

Persephone provides images of the central mystery of the female psyche as it deals with the archetypal polarity of the Mother and Kore. Archetypal polarities are connected along a continuum, which is how Jung positions the Kore as counterpart to the Mother: "The figure corresponding to the Kore in a woman is generally double one, i.e. a mother and a maiden, which is to say that she appears now as the one, now as the other."[233] For Jung, the Kore finds her 'other' not in a negative or dark Kore aspect, but in the Mother. As a woman's unconscious is structured by these two archetypes, the Kore and Mother form the essential polarity that expresses the entirety of a woman's psychic character. Together they "extend the feminine consciousness both upwards and downwards,"[234] down into the ancestral realm and up into the immortality that the future promises. Jung's point is that these archetypal entities co-exist in the psyche, allowing a woman to embrace both, not only sequentially but simultaneously, assuming, as just discussed, they have been well differentiated. We could also interpret this same continuum biologically as the pattern playing out between generations where life flows from mother to daughter. For where the Mother points back to the ancestors, the Kore points forward to the next generation.

That Persephone has no children shows how Kore transformation is not in the fertility of Mother goddesses but in an interiority. Because Kore processes of transformation deal with the articulation of one's vitality and beingness, they are invisible, belonging partly to the underworld and its values. This is exquisitely captured by Rilke in his poem on Orpheus and Eurydice. Descending to the underworld to retrieve his dead bride, Orpheus attains his aim but ultimately fails to bring her back to life by looking over his shoulder. In the final moments of their doomed ascent, Rilke describes Eurydice walking behind Orpheus,

She was inside herself, like a great hope,
and never thought of the man who walked ahead
or the road that climbed back toward life.
She was inside herself. And her being dead
filled her like tremendous depth.
As a fruit is filled with its sweetness and darkness

she was filled with her big death, still so new
that it hadn't been fathomed.
She found herself in a resurrected
virginity.[235]

Eurydice and Persephone articulate the underworld values that belong to Kore creativity which include soulmaking through solitude, renewal through falling apart, dedication, staying connected to those essential patterns of psychic life and their images, and a concern with ritual. Perhaps then for the Kore, this continuum of feminine creativity that Jung describes could be understood in terms of types of verticality: downwards to the earthy matter of the body (Mother) and upwards to the creative impulses of the spirit (Kore); downwards into the imaginal realm of the soul where lunar waters fall (Kore) and upward to the generativity that is nourished by rich soil and solar warmth (Mother). Where the Mother's fecund creativity moves outward in the generation of life, the Kore's creativity moves inwardly. Korehood blossoms below ground. We leave Mother and Kore separate so that psychologically a woman can live both.

My aim has been to pay careful attention to Persephone, the configurations she appears in and the changes she undergoes, in order to discover constellations of Kore consciousness. It is crucial that we begin to see the Kore in relationship to the Mother. Psychologically, this means a more differentiated and conscious relation to each aspect, allowing one to stand more squarely in the outer roles and expressions of each end of the continuum, the mothering position and the independent virgin presence.

When we remain unconscious, the psychological dominance of the Mother archetype robs us of a plurality of figures that comprise our inner psychic landscapes and myths. On the other side of this sleepy cohesion deeper stirrings in the psyche reveal changes are afoot. As Jane Hollister Wheelwright observed, the ideal of the Great Mother no longer holds women's psyches the way it had for many centuries:

The female unconscious being now interested in a more ageless, more ideal and mysterious figure of the female aspect of the Self than the old Earth Mother who, because of patriarchal domination, became less comprehensive. [This shift] is bound to help bring back the concept of the Maiden... Modern young women, if they are honest, can recognize for themselves the multiplicity of the female self.[236]

As the old archetype begins to loosen its grip, women are seeking a more complex, multifaceted image of their deep nature. This promising future goes hand in hand with the development of the Kore-Virgin aspect of their psychic character.

By identifying the barrier that the Mother can erect against the differentiation that is necessary to Kore consciousness, the Kore-Mother archetypal continuum can be reimagined as a simultaneously new and ancient kind of synchrony. Our task is to cultivate our consciousness of, and relationship to, the Kore, for she holds the key to the rejuvenation of the principles that are so needed. A connection to these two archetypal rhythms is what give women grounding in their psyches—the Kore may then symbolize a future that is simultaneously linked to the ancestral past via the Mother. It is the Kore who oversees our deepest rhythms in the midst of the changes and challenges that our inner and outer lives demand. The woman who makes a place for Persephone invites an understanding of how separation from the Mother and underworld descent leads to the articulation of one's sovereign and whole being.

Korai Triad Goddesses

—

CHAPTER NINE

Korai Triad Goddesses

And their feet move
rhythmically, as tender
feet of Cretan girls
danced once around an
altar of love, crushing
a circle in the soft
smooth flowering grass

Sappho

The mythic imagination reveals the soul's complexity. The sufferings, raptures, and transformations depicted in myth are metaphors given by the psyche, an imaginative process evident since the beginning of human consciousness across cultures and time. We might say myth is the soul's poem, composed for the many yet inscribed upon each individual heart. The universality of their metaphors is shown by the myths themselves, having survived from oral traditions, pictorial representations, and texts.

The creation of the cosmos and the birth of the gods are two fundamental occurrences in all mythologies. In Greek myth, we can trace the way each generation of gods reflects a different cosmos, and such cosmologies in turn ensoul every quarter of life. The more immediate topography of myth also parallels that of the soul, from the depths of Hades to the vault of Olympus, extending to the Elysian fields and craggy peaks of Mount Parnassus, occupying palaces and the sheepfolds of every village, marked by each Hecatean crossroad and temple ground. Both the gods and their realms mirror the archetypal depths of our being.

In Greek myth there are perhaps hundreds of groups of sister goddesses and nymphs, and very few groups of brother gods. It is quite startling when one begins to notice just how often feminine figures appear in groups while masculine figures tend towards dyads or are solitary. The triple form grouping is unique to Kore-Virgin goddesses; there are no equivalent male triad gods in Greek myth. This point of distinction cannot be underestimated. Furies, Fates, Graces, Hours, Graiai, Sirens and Thriai—who are these Korai? What are their qualities and characteristics? In what ways are these divinities animated by the Kore archetype and its themes, and how do these figures deepen the inquiry into archetypal virginity or korehood? As triad sisters, what do they make visible about the archetypal field of sisterhood?

The great goddesses of ancient traditions whose virginal being was venerated are psychological images of that essential aspect of the psyche that is unto-herself. This at-one-ment of our essential nature is expressed in sovereignty, independence, and integrity, qualities central to the Kore archetype. I showed in Part I how we are in touch with the Kore whenever we're living from the ground of our own values, ideals, and emotional reality. Discerning and articulating this ground can also be understood as contact with an incorruptible value, the experience of having something in yourself that, no matter what happens, cannot be taken from you. Unto-herself and sovereign, the Kore-Virgin carries a sense of intrinsic, irreducible worth that translates to a sense of equality in the world based on the value of one's being.

While the essence of the Kore is this at-one-ment, the group identity of the triad goddesses has always been more evident than their individuality. As sisters, the Korai triads are one and many, individuals and an intimately related multiplicity. Physical plurality, fluid boundaries, and relational permeability are intertwined in these figures, which returns us to the psychological theme of women's interior multiplicity. Jane Hollister Wheelwright and Irene Claremont De Castillejo both noticed in their work with women that Maiden-Virgin soul figures appear in plural forms. As was discussed in Part I in relationship to Persephone as Kore, Hollister Wheelwright showed how the Maiden archetype is multivalent, appearing as young girl, lover, sister, and this was reiterated in the examples De Castillejo drew from her client's imaginal work. The triad Korai sisters figuratively illustrate this paradox of the Kore archetype, the simultaneous expression of individuality and multiplicity.

All the triad goddesses are Kore in the same way as Artemis and Athena—for all are Virgins, *parthenos*, unmarried and unto-themselves. They are also all childless.[237] All are sovereign and active divinities in the Greek mythological cosmos, moving both independently and in relationship to other gods and figures.

In mythological scholarship, many of the Korai triads have been sourced back to older dualities or pairs of goddesses, or seen as derivative, or more articulated emanations of a greater goddess, such as the Graces in relationship to Aphrodite.[238] Undoubtedly, the relationships the triad goddesses have to other divinities shines a light on their psychological configurations. While these lineages offer insights, to really comprehend the triads means staying close to their essential imaginal representation rather than folding them into another archetypal figure.

Like the principles or powers belonging to any of the divinities, those of the triad goddesses are also incorruptible and pure, meaning they cannot be impinged upon. The gods are born and impose a principle upon the world, one that must be yielded to. In other words, they personify archetypal laws and are beyond allegory. The principled stance is very much what the Kore archetype signifies. While these general factors connect the triad goddesses to the Kore archetype, the specific principles they stand for amplify the Kore in distinct ways.

I have come to understand the triad goddesses as iconoclastic of feminine archetypes, in the sense that they are direct and sustain a quality of opening. Openings bespeak possibilities, which is one of the most signal features of archetypes. In Hillman's words, "Archetypes are the skeletal structures of the psyche, yet the bones are changeable constellations of light - sparks, waves, motions. They are principles of uncertainty."[239] Representing particular principles, the Korai triads are best understood as analogies of the psyche. Fate (the Fates), grace (the Graces), atonement (the Furies)—these are fields of experience corresponding to what lives between consciousness and unconsciousness, where life pulls you *into* the experience of fate, or processes of atonement. Thus the triads feed the mind in a more immediate way than the goddesses and gods who require a seeing through to their metaphorical resonances. The goddesses and gods—Aphrodite, Artemis, Hermes—are metaphors because they have these personified lives that we have to translate to the universal patterns of the psyche, whereas the triads already constellate around a principle, a psychological current of life that is named.

It is not that the triad goddesses do not belong to the imagination; it is that they have one foot in the imagination and one foot in the necessity of our awakening. They are archetypal principles that are also pushing us towards the reflexive achievements of civilization. It's as though the triads work psychologically like the anima and animus that Jung and Jungians describe as complexes *and* archetypes which awaken us to the autonomy of the psyche. Hence, they are figures that bridge the personal psyche and collective psyche. Do we not experience fate as both a personal and impersonal force? Atonement by definition has to relate to our subjective experience and at the same time to something larger than us. The triads occupy this bridging role in the psyche that serve as conduits to the deeper archetypal world.

Over the many years I've shared my work on these triad goddesses I've been asked the same question, *Why are they three*? In the Western tradition, three has conveyed the dynamism of life for millennia. Three is symbolic of flow, movement and change. This religious idea, Marija Gimbutas argues, originated in the Paleolithic era and has been constant throughout prehistoric and historic European and Mediterranean mythological systems.[240] So it's fitting there would be so many goddesses as they personify the dynamic forces to which life is beholden. At the same time, we have to bear in mind that, as Renaissance scholar Edgar Wind remarked, "A myth gets its animation from a mystery."[241]

CHAPTER TEN

Graces or Charities

If there is any characteristic that most evidently appears to carry divinity in it, it is gracefulness. Whether a human trait or a psychological experience, grace is that ineffable quality that most clearly reveals the presence of something numinous. From the Greek verb *charein* "to rejoice," *charis* means "grace or kindness," and its origin lies in the Indo-European root for pleasure.[242] The Charities, who we've come to know as the Graces— Aglaia "Splendid Beauty," Euphrosyne "Mirthful, Good Cheer," and Thalia "Abundance, Plenty"—personify this encounter with transcendent beauty and grace. Their arrival is analogous to those times when we feel ourselves the recipient of a divine kindness or the beholder of extraordinary beauty. An ancient ode to the Graces affirms this, "For in your gift are all our mortal joys, and every sweet thing, be it wisdom, beauty, or glory, that makes rich the soul of man."[243]

The Graces were born from the union of briny depths and heavenly peaks. Their mother Eurynome was one of the most ancient oceanic goddesses, and their father was Zeus. Possible depictions of Eurynome are limited to what has been found at her temple in Arcadia, where there is a cult image of a woman with a fish's tail who is draped in gold chains.[244] Hesiod says that originally she ruled from Olympus with Ophim before the Titans, Kronos and Rhea. Later they came to make their home in Okeanos, thenceforth called the Old Ones of the Sea.

The Graces have been dancing with clasped hands since the archaic period in Greece, as early as the eighth century BCE. Lovers of song, they often dance with the nine Muses and Artemis to Apollo's music. It was said that the gods can neither feast nor dance without them, they who bring "enchantment, splendor, lightness, and festive joy and merriment."[245] Thus they were known as the "stewards of all rites of heaven,"[246] ensuring that the gods take delight in each other's company. This mutual warmth is what classicist Bonnie McLachlan describes as the pleasure-bearing power of *charis,* which occurs when we are generous in giving to another, and in that giving we experience pleasure.[247] This harmonious flow of giving and receiving is personified by the dancing Graces. The beauty of this mutuality lies at the root of charity (*caritas*) as Christian love and benevolent goodwill.

The beauty in giving pleasure to another, as well as being magnanimous for another's benefit and care is expressed by the Graces close relationship to Aphrodite. Her power, Hillman says, is felt "as an aesthetic intensity that takes hold like a moral force, an obligation to notice and respond,"[248] and reveals the depth of the soul's longing for beauty. The Graces are skilled in the making of Aphrodite's luxurious garments including her grey *peplum* (shawl), and they are adept in the art of cosmetics and adornments that are among this goddess' tools. When Aphrodite falls in love with Anchises, she retreats to her temple in Cyprus to prepare herself for their love affair, and there "the Graces bathed her with heavenly oils such as blooms upon the bodies of the eternal gods—oil divinely sweet, which she had by her, filled with fragrance."[249] In Hesiod's telling, the Graces, Hours, and Persuasion—the closest of Aphrodite's companions—clothed and adorned the exquisitely crafted Pandora.

Hesiod said that from the gaze of the Graces "flowed love that unnerves the limbs: and beautiful is their glance beneath their brows."[250] Their beauty arrests and loosens at one and the same time. Related to the verb *chairein,* which connotes something that shines or glitters, their eyes emit a light that further emphasizes their captivating nature.[251] Persephone's annual path up from Hades is said to be illuminated by this light from their eyes. The blossoming earth that would greet the ascending goddesses expresses the mutual receptivity that marks *charis*, that quality Walter Otto said is the most beautiful of all, the "charm that reveals itself or opens itself up to the heart."[252]

We can see how grace was understood by the Greeks as that which is pleasurable in terms of the feeling quality it bestows rather than as a thing in and of itself. Plato said *charis* is a "divine delicateness and extreme tenderness since its nature is fluctuating and flexible, [thus] it penetrates or slips imperceptibly into the soul."[253] I think this is felt when we come into alignment with the gods. We could say that to be fully human, but to live in accord with the will of the gods, is to be full of grace, which is itself ever fluctuating and flexible. Yet throughout our life we find ourselves in service to certain gods, for life seems to require that particular divinities receive our attention at different times and in various circumstances. This is what Hillman means when he says how, "it is important, in our daily troubles, to know from whom the troubles come," and to ask not *what* to do with the problem or pain, "but rather: To what God or Goddess do I sacrifice in this situation? If you know which mythical pattern, which archetypal drama, is being enacted in your dilemma you are already on the road to relief."[254] To engage in these questions is to invite that quality of consciousness that the Graces personify, as they have to do with living a life attuned to the soul.

Our alignment with the gods is made evident in simple ways, too, as when we take notice of someone's smooth and graceful physicality, or by paying attention to how someone deftly navigates an awkward situation we acknowledge the optimal handling as if they were divinely touched or inspired. Whether psychological or physical, grace is experienced as something fluid and smooth and "is never associated with constraint or affectation; it is elusive and light, and it acts in the simplicity and calmness of the soul; it avoids violent passions," writes classicist Raffaelle Milani.[255] Understood in this way, the power of the Graces' beauty is felt as a sense of well-being. This leads back to the larger theme of Kore integrity, that quality of connection one has to the deeper life principles to which one is beholden.

The spiritual nature of grace, the deep well-being we experience as a gift, coming as it were from the heavens, finds expression in the myths and rituals belonging to the Graces. From Orchomenos, an ancient center of Mycenaean civilization, comes record from the second century BCE of the cult worship of the Graces.[256] According to the geographer Pausanias, this temple contained three stones which fell from heaven upon which were images of the goddesses. King Eteocles received these sky-fallen gifts and made the first sacrifices to the Graces, and his three daughters, the Trittai, performed a dance in their honor.[257] Tragedy struck during their dance and the Trittai fell into a well and died. In mourning, the goddess Gaia created a flower in their name that has three parts.[258] Kerényi makes a fascinating observation that the Graces and Trittai are two forms of the same divine power: "The story of the three stones that fell from heaven preserved the memory of their heavenly origin, whereas the story of their disappearance in a well preserved their connection with the deep waters and the underworld."[259] By being paired with the Trittai, the lesser known origin of the Graces' is brought to light, for some say they are daughters of Nyx or Lethe, both are underworld goddesses.

This idea that grace is born in the underworld rounds out the figures of the Graces and suggests that grace is not just in the province of the heavenly gods above, but can equally originate from below in the depths. In other words, grace is not only a spiritual matter but arises in the place of one's rootedness. Grace from the realm below would mean approaching the realm as Hillman did, seeing it as the place of soul making. The qualities he ascribes to the soul, this ineffable factor that is a perspective rather than a substance, is an underworld vision or deepening viewpoint, "which makes meaning possible, turns events into experiences."[260] This gives the circumstances of our lives, the issues of our character, and the difficulties that give shape to our fate, a hidden purpose. This unseen aspect of psychic life and our afflictions, is what makes the unfathomable underworld depths the soul's place as well as its way of seeing.

The underworld origin of the Graces shows the grace of a soul perspective. It is the suppleness of imaginal possibility in those areas of our lives that have grown old and inflexible, our consciousness caught in outworn stories. It is the grace that comes when we trust our afflictions to be openings for soul. This netherworld beauty of the Graces would also be that sense of connection that comes when we engage in reflective awareness. This requires a certain receptivity rather than active striving for clarity. It is from a lunar reflective eye that we glimpse an image, hear the chord, or feel the thread the psyche has spun connecting us to some truth that belongs to the ground of our being.

For Kerényi, the Graces falling from heaven illustrates how the gift of grace is the most *naturally* spiritual of experiences.[261] With the power to nourish the parched soul, grace is often likened to rain. A Hindu wisdom saying puts it thus, "The grace of God is coming down upon us all the time, like a gentle rain, but we forget to cup our hands."[262] Emotional pain, spiritual crisis, and profound loss arrive with great burdens for our hearts and we often harden in response to their weight. It is into these petrified places that grace flows. The well-worn words of master bard Leonard Cohen remind us that it is through the cracks that the light gets in.[263] Grace is the light that finds its way into the hardness of our depressions and dis-ease, into the fissures of our complexes. This reconnection to the vital waters that flow through life means coming into alignment with these goddesses whose presence restores psychic movement. The flow of the Graces' threefold rhythm shows grace as the smooth joining together of us to the gods in the mutuality of *charis*, the harmonious accord of giving and receiving. That this is natural, full with its own ease, and moves in accord with the mysterious laws of the psyche is perhaps what it is to be in a state of grace.

Hours or Horai

Seasons have their own character. Whether of the natural outer world or inner landscape, time is a qualitative phenomenon. We speak of times of year that are sweet and mild, others that are sharp and demanding, noticing how the sun's light is fierce in summer, and golden soft in autumn. The metaphors of nature connect us to the deeper rhythms of the life of the psyche. In winter periods we are quiet, as though our ground is snow-laden and outward movement limited. The psyche slumbers, resting and breathing into its fallowness. These are times of waiting, dreaming, incubating. Eventually seeds crack open and life pushes its way up through the patient fields, sprouting roots downward while simultaneously pushing upward in search of sunlight. New energy, new ideas, new life always emerge after periods of barrenness and dormancy.

In the mythic imagination, the Hours personify this archetypally patterned flow of nature, its regular phases and seasonal processes of birth, growth, and decay. Daughters of the Titan goddess Themis, "law of nature" and Zeus's first wife, these Kore goddesses are Eunomia "Right Order," clear-eyed Dike "Justice," and blooming Eirene "Peace".[264]

Horai, Greek for Hours, comes from the root *hora*, which means "the correct moment." Thus the Hours have the power to "bring and bestow ripeness."[265] The right moment is qualitatively ripe. When we're attuned to the distinctive rhythms of time, we're able to move and respond to life in accord with a deeper flow. This feeling for the psychological nature of time and right timing is the core of Hours consciousness. Personifying "a rhythm in the time-flow of things,"[266] as expressed in the hours of the day and the seasons of the year, their names—Right Order, Justice, and Peace—reveal how these principles underlie the order of the macrocosm and find their parallel in our daily lives. This time-flow awareness is an antidote to the one-sided busyness that characterizes our contemporary Western world. While ego strength and will are necessary means for progress and achievement of our goals, and this orientation to life in pursuit of one's needs and desires is required for success in collective terms, it can overwhelm the sensitivity that is tuned into questions of right timing.

The seasonal flow of the natural world is based on laws of energy that underlie the psyche. Knowing when the time is ripe to rest and therefore say *no* to a new project, or leap on in, requires reflection. A connection to the Hours means being attentive to our inner sense of right time, an attunement to the rhythmic periods of nature. Determining this has become challenging with the widespread embrace of growth through productivity, 24/7 connectivity and endless doing. Standing up against this pressure, internally and externally, is never easy, but it's the primary position of the Kore who stands for integrity to one's nature. Discernment is key, and like Psyche, we learn to sort and separate the heaping muchness of life, becoming aware of what matters by differentiating through careful, diligent, antlike attention what is true for us and therefore what is ultimately valuable and what is not.

In discussing this rhythmic flow and attunement, I am aware of how occupying this state can arise as an idealized goal—the notion we can become untouchable (psychologically virginal) despite familial, social, and cultural pressures to be certain ways, or that we can be always be at peace, and that the rhythms of the psyche are coherent to consciousness. We saw how the desire to remain inviolable belongs to the shadow side of the Kore. Myth depicts this fundamental tension that belongs to the archetype in this respect, for the Hours are often depicted in opposition to forces that threatens to undo them. Dike is dragging or beating Adikia "Injustice," and Eirene and Eunomia are opposed by Polemos "War" and Dysnomia "Lawlessness." Similarly, when we're concerned with the orderedness of life, concern for its opposite is implied, for there is a relationship between order and chaos, peace and mayhem, justice and injustice. Awareness of the possible undoing of our inner order keeps us related to the Kore. It is she who brings a sense of renewal, the possibility of a new start when things have gone awry and need reorientation.

Returning to their power to bestow ripeness, it is the Hours who greet Aphrodite when she first comes to shore after rising from the white foam of the sea. Adorning her with gold jewels and clothing her in fine linen, they ripen Aphrodite's beauty by adding value to it. Of their gifts Hillman writes,

> these jeweled intricacies are human constructs that mimic, in human mode, the inventions of nature, like the light on the water of sea, the flavors of rain—all that brings to display the Goddess's beauty, so that her being is not merely a principle of aesthetics or a metaphysical force of passion permeating the entire cosmos called eros or libido or *jouissance* or love, but beauty as *exact particulars of sensuous display* in each moment of each hour, revealing, in one and the same instant, fittingness, the rightful place, a delightful justness, the pleasure of order.[267]

Safran E mail

The sensuous particularities that enhance beauty can be understood as a ripening of nature, a fulfilling of its essence. Clothing, jewelry, makeup can all be imagined as ripening agents of natural beauty and form, the gifts of these goddesses. It is Hours consciousness that knows the right details and the correct composition that enhance the beauty of the world.

As the practice of astrology is concerned with the harmonious and orderly movement of the celestial bodies and their correspondence in human lives, it is in this practice that we can also come in contact with Hours consciousness. Calendrical celebrations of time, whether of the sun's annual movement through the zodiac, new moons, the solstice and equinox points, these orientations mark the movement of the cosmos in relation to the movement of the soul. An astrology that focuses on the symbolic level reveals its concern for the archetypal energies of the psyche as they appear in outer planetary bodies and their inner psychological configurations. This understanding, based on the ancient vision of a cosmos wherein "all things breathe together," as Plotinus remarked, expresses the Hours interest in the deep patterns along which life unfolds.

Order, justice, and peace are results of living in accord with natural laws, yet they are also the ideal ordering principles of civilization, which deals with the complicated reality of living together, gods and mortals alike. Each of the Hours are concerned with this issue of right relationship, giving a more particular articulation to the natural laws of their mother Themis. Bright Themis, a goddess of the celestial realm, is the voice of divine law. As mother of the Fates and Hours, Themis personifies the fabric that binds the gods. She is the divine order of nature which Kerényi characterizes as the norm of all beings living together; the rules of conduct between women and men as well as gods and mortals long established by custom and tradition. Her laws are distinct from those of human decree which are called *nomos*. Though Themis is easy to obey she "also forbids many things,"[268] and these are the most foundational precepts to which all beings must submit, the laws of nature that all beings must live within. One way that the laws of the gods are communicated to mortals is through oracles, and originally it was Themis who presided over these ancient places, including Delphi. (We will return to Themis and oracular knowledge in discussion of the Thriai.)

Differentiating their mother's principles in the world, the Hours, according to Pindar, are the "support of cities" and "stewards of wealth for mankind."[269] Their powers are related to the human and divine realm of laws, and deal with issues of social prosperity. This is evinced in their role as protectors; it is said that when the Kouretes were shielding the infant Zeus from Kronos, they sang hymns to the Hours for their protection. This also helps make sense of their position as wardens of the gates of Olympus, which they fiercely protected during the Titanomachy, the epic battle between the Olympians and the Titans.

Hesiod tells us that Dike sits beside Zeus and gives him counsel, because she joins dissimilars through the equality of truth.[270] Dike knows how to bring together what is at odds by identifying what is just. It's said that this goddess abandoned earth during the Civilization of Iron, the last and darkest of the four mythic ages marked by violence and greed.[271] In despair of humankind's debasement of justice, honor, and love, Dike turned herself into the stars that form the constellation Virgo, the Virgin. Eunomia "reveals all that is orderly and fitting" and "makes the rough smooth, puts a stop to excess, weakens insolence, dries up the blooming of ruin, straightens out crooked judgements, tames deeds of pride."[272] She sets right the shape and order of things that have become imbalanced through excessive growth, and brings our attention to the wisdom of the middle path that lies between extremes. Last there is peaceful Eirene, the nurse of children and beloved of families. Ovid called her great mother to Demeter, and portrayed this goddess of the grain suckling at Eirene's breast—the nourishing bounty of the fields is itself nurtured by social and political peace.[273]

Thriai

Divination is a way of establishing connection between the realm of the gods and the human world. In its practice, certain actions, symbols, or words can become ways of opening the door to the divine world. In every symptom, conflict, or problem, there is a god attempting to communicate with us. As Jung famously stated, "the gods have become diseases."[274] So when we turn to divination such as archetypal astrology, the I Ching, or tarot for counsel in our predicament or confusion, we are endeavoring to find that god and to turn our problem over to something greater than ourselves.

Divination thus gives voice to what is unknown or in the shadow of a situation. By bringing up what is hidden, we can connect to the images, stories, and spiritual principles that we cannot see from our current conscious perspective. The encounter with what has been unconscious changes us by affecting our attitude toward the situation and how we see ourselves. Understood in this way, divination is not about ascertaining the future, rather it is a mode of opening up to the synchronistic appearance of significances that impel us to reflect on the issue at hand in a deeper way. In this manner divination becomes an opening into a psychological response to our situation, and the psyche, as Hillman says, "favors responses in metaphors, images, sharp-pointed insights that stir the mind to awakened observation and deepened reflection."[275] Divination's imaginal way of knowing opens us up to something new. This receptivity to the unknown is the territory of the Kore whose youthful vitality inspires a renewal of vision whereby everything is seen afresh and full of possibility.

The connection between divination and the archetypal Kore is most apparent in the Thriai, goddesses whose divinatory arts are much praised by Apollo and Hermes. Directly figuring in no myths, the little we know about these Korai goddesses comes directly from Apollo:

> There are certain holy ones, sisters born—three virgins gifted with wings: their heads are besprinkled with white meal, and they dwell under a ridge of Parnassos. These are teachers of divination apart from me, the art which I practised while yet a boy following herds, though my father paid no heed to it. From their home they fly now here, now there, feeding on honey-comb and bringing all things to pass. And when they are inspired through eating yellow honey, they are willing to speak the truth; but if they be deprived of the gods' sweet food, then they speak falsely, as they swarm in

and out together. These, then, I give you; enquire of them strictly and delight your heart: and if you should teach any mortal so to do often will he hear your response—if he have good fortune.[276]

Apollo calls these maiden goddesses with bees' wings "teachers of divination," and the secret to their manner of instruction lies before our eyes—it is the Kore's receptivity to the vital streams of life that makes them permeable to the knowledge of the gods which confers divinatory insight, direction, and wisdom.

In the Greek tradition, oracular speech was the domain of virgin priestesses whose art was rendering the signs of the gods truly and faithfully. In the classical tradition, divination and oracular knowledge were Apollo's domain, whose hallowed sanctuary of Delphi was home to the Pythian priestess. However, in the earlier strata of mythic history, the gift of oracular speech began with the goddess Ge, the primordial and chthonic earth. Before Apollo's ascent in the Olympian pantheon, it was from Ge that the fumes arose in the temple of Delphi, which the Pythia would inhale while sitting on the sacred tripod. Ge then gave the oracle to her daughter Themis, goddess of eternal law, so it was originally passed through the motherline, making the prophetic language of the oracular tradition originally feminine.[277]

The fifth-century Vulci Cup provides one of the only ancient depictions of an oracular consultation. The goddess Themis is seated on a tripod holding a spray of laurel and a *phiale* or shallow libation bowl. Before her stands Aegeus, the childless King of Athens who went to Delphi to learn when he was to have a son. Divine prophetess, Themis is the voice of oracular truth that provides wise counsel as long as the words are properly understood. Hearing the voice of divine laws as opposed to human decrees requires a special kind of listening, for like myth, Themis's knowledge is communicated in metaphors. Aegeus could not understand the meaning of her message, and unable to heed the knowledge it offered, unwittingly incited a long series of tragic events.

It's a metaphorical sensibility that understands the as-if nature of the psyche's language, hearing words as guides that open up a path of understanding rather than as mists that obscure it. Apollo says that when the Thriai are deprived of their oracular honey food, they will speak oracles that are untrue, so to have their aid they must be fed what is carefully gathered and prepared. This means that to hear an insightful message, we have to be attentive and feed the psyche the right food. I take this to mean that by paying attention to our dreams and divination practices, and working with the material symbolically, the psyche is given the nourishment it needs. And if deprived of the gods' sweet food, the words spoken are misheard, taken literally, reduced to one level of meaning, or egoically focused. Aegeus shows how the message that is not understood may as well be a false message, because no insight or understanding can come of it.

The contemplative strength of the Kore is key for any work that touches into the unconscious. Marion Woodman connects this core understanding of the Virgin's power back to her essential one-in-herselfness. The capacity to contain is what allows one to connect with the images that arise from the psyche and work them into life. The Kore personifies the ability to bridge the unconscious and conscious through symbolic contemplation. Strong and flexible enough to be in contact with the psyche's depths, "the virgin's meditative strength is crucial in individual rituals,"[278] says Woodman, for it keeps the ego from becoming inflated and then confused and scared.

Kore containment allows one to become a vessel for the divine. This capacity for vesseling the god or spirit is conveyed in different ways in the mythic history of the Pythian priestess. In her study of virginity in the classical Greek world, Classicist Guilia Sissa discusses how in the older traditions where oracles were the messages of the goddesses Ge and Themis, the Pythia was virgin not in the sexual sense but *parthenos* in that she knew that transmission of the goddesses messages required purity of expression. The priestess was called a "woman of silence,"[279] indicating that she knew when a virginal silence on behalf of the gods was required. In other words, she knew when not to speak.

When Apollo took control of the oracle at Delphi by slaying the pythian serpent who was the chthonic embodiment of the powers of Ge and Themis, the meaning and role of the priestesses virginity changed. Sissa addresses the differences noting how the "sexual aspect of virginity is most specific and pertinent in the priestesses relations with a male god, [whereas] the woman who is the earth's spokesperson is virgin with respect to her mouth."[280] That Apollo required sexual virginity in his priestess so that her purity was his alone, reveals how desire was a "fundamental constant in Apollo's relations with his prophetesses."[281] As the incarnate vessel for his power, it was his voice that came through her body. In a kind of sacred union, the priestess and god became one and like a reed she carried his message, or like a lover his divine seed. These facets of the ancient Greek oracular tradition show the Kore's containment in both the Pythian priestess, whose virginity symbolized her capacity to render the gods' messages clear and true, and the mantic powers of the Thriai. These Korai are in our attunement to the metaphor-rich psychic food that we need, and those practices that provide such nourishment.

CHAPTER ELEVEN

Fates or Moirai

For the ancient Greeks, one's fate was shaped and guided by the Fates—the fingers of inscrutable Clotho "the Spinner," Lachesis "the Apportioner," and Atropos "She who Cannot be Turned." Though these goddesses were rarely individualized in terms of personality or physical distinction, in Hesiod's *Shield of Herakles* it is said that though Atropos is shorter and older than her two sisters, to her goes the greatest honor and highest ranking.[282] Moirai comes from *moira* meaning parts, shares, or allotted portions, and these three goddesses are the ones who spin the lots of life. That all living beings are subject to the Fates, who are older and more powerful than any of the gods, means we are all accountable to fate—limited to the portion of life that is ours with its bounds and inevitable end.

There are three mother-lines belonging to the Fates, each one personifying a principle of cosmic order. Like the Hours, they were known as the daughters of Themis, goddess of the eternal laws of nature. But they were also daughters of Nyx,[283] the goddess of the primordial night from which the cosmos emerged, and Ananke "Necessity." Ananke is among the cosmic forces that form the nature of the universe. She was central for Plato, the *axis mundi* in his "Myth of Er," wherein he described how it is upon her wide lap that the spindle that shapes the threads of our

FATES

lives is formed.[284] Hillman says that it is this goddess who, "establishes what the soul has selected for its lot to be necessary—not an accident, not good or bad, not foreknown or guaranteed, simply necessary."[285] Seated around her throne are her daughters the Fates, singing as they aid her in the mysterious working of a life's essential shape.

The Greeks understood fate as that which binds us to the laws of nature, of which we all have a part. So rather than being goddesses who dispense gifts and curses, rendering free will impotent, the Fates are guardians of our deep nature. This understanding has undergone much change in the Western worldview, to be now nearly incomprehensible except for a few fields that connect deep character with outer events, including depth psychology and archetypal astrology. In *The Astrology of Fate*, Jungian analyst and astrologer Liz Greene discusses the major influences and attitudes to which we owe our current thinking on fate. Among the most important paradigm shifts began during the Reformation which saw major changes in religion, science and philosophy. This period saw the ascendancy of the rational mind over nature, the consequence of which was a loss of our sense of connection to Nature and natural law, an inheritance that has us believe that we are living above Nature's necessities by virtue of our minds. We've forgotten the meaning of fate and how it shows up in the simple facts of life and death, something we see at work in the field of post-humanism which envisions a future where humans meld with machines and escape Nature's laws all together. Greene writes that fate has come to "imply a loss of control, a sense of powerlessness, impotence and humiliation."[286] In other words, fate has developed into fatalism, the abdication of personal responsibility and the powerlessness of free will. Her view of how the idea of fate sits in our psyche today provides critical insight into the issue:

> Fate means: it has been written. For something to be written with such immovability by an utterly unseen hand is a terrifying thought. It implies not only powerlessness, but the dark machinery of some vast impersonal Wheel or highly ambiguous God which takes less account than we would like of our hopes, dreams, desires, loves, merits or even our

sins. Of what value are the individual's efforts, his moral struggles, his humble acts of love and courage, his strivings for the betterment of himself and his family and his world, if all is ultimately rendered pointless by what has already been written? We have been fed, for the last two centuries, on a highly questionable pabulum of rational self-determi- nation, and such a vision of fate threatens an experience of real despair, or a chaotic abreaction where the spinal column of the mortal and ethical man collapses. There is equally a difficulty with the more mystical approach to fate, for by severing the unity of body and spirit in order to seek refuge from the strictures of fate, the individual creates an artificial dissociation from his own natural law, and may invoke in the outer world what he is avoiding in the inner.[287]

In naming the existential anxiety the idea of fate breeds, Greene brings clarity to the issues implicit in our Western rationalistic and deterministic worldview. When we turn to the wisdom of the Greeks and their sense of the deep and mysterious issue of fate, we find something very different from the fatalism or spiritual transcendence that arise as compensations to this view.

The Greek philosopher Anaximander understood Moira as an eternal motion within the cosmos from which the universe receives its elemental divisions.[288] These divisions include life's rhythms, and as we are part of a cosmic motion, to be in accord with this divine order means to flow with the shape of our fate. Anyone who has worked with textiles knows what it feels like to find our rhythm with the materials, the wool trans-forming through our fingers via the kinetic energy of the spindle, the knitting needles looping orchestration, the swift embroidery stitch rising and falling like a ship upon a linen sea. Here be the Fates, their dancing hands drawing and sharing the thread of each life.

In her retelling of the myth of Theseus, novelist Mary Renault describes Moira as, "The finished shape of our fate, the line drawn round it. It is the task the gods allot us, and the share of glory they allow; the limits we must not pass; and our appointed end. Moira is all these."[289] Our share of

myth of Theseus re Moira

glory in life is our distinguishing quality or ability. To the extent that we attend to that gift, we are participating in a larger order of which we are a part. While glory has become synonymous with fame, for the ancients this pertained to the nature of one's character and its full blossoming or shining in life. This is what Heraclitus meant when he said *character is fate*, for who we are is intertwined with what will unfold. In this sense, then, our glory can be our warmheartedness, our silvery quick tongue, our gentleness of spirit that puts others at ease, or our depth of character. "What determines eminence," Hillman writes, "is less a call to greatness than the call of character, that inability to be other than what you are in acorn, following it faithfully or being desperately driven by its dream."[290]

Our share of eminence is what connects us to the gods, but it is limited and in that sense warns against inflation. We need to be vivified by the gods but not identify with them and exceed our limits. Being aware of our allotted portion in life means not overstepping our bounds and having a sense of *right measure*. Understood in this way, rather than being a force that narrowly predetermines or dictates one's actions, fate is concerned with the contours and limitations, the order of Nature within which gods and mortals cohabitate. The Fates are the guardians of the boundaries of each person's fate, the limits that must not be passed, because to transgress these bounds would be to disturb these goddesses who will exact penalty for any transgression. When we turn our back on the actuality of circumstance, it is like trying to escape our fate. Then it often seems that fate comes in with a heavy hand. It's as if the Fates become angry when we don't follow or obey the laws of our deep nature.

For Plotinus, particularity is an essential feature of fate. The distinctiveness that characterizes a person comes with a deep appreciation of the unique givens of circumstance. Such appreciation allows one to stay within the bounds of one's lot.[291] We can say that to work with what is given is the work of individuation, which means facing up to one's talents and calling (the glories), wounds, and eccentricities. Returning to Heraclitus's axiom that character is fate, to know our character is to have an easier time with our necessity. This sense of being at ease with fate goes hand in hand with a feeling of integrity, and it is this that connects it to the Kore pattern. Integrity means living within our bounds and cultivating the particularities of our nature; it means being aligned with our deeper character.

Hillman draws out another aspect of the Fates: "Moira derives from the root *smer* or *mer*, meaning to ponder, to think, to meditate, consider, care. It is a deeply psychological term requiring us to scrutinize events with respect to the portion that comes from elsewhere and is unaccountable, and the portion that belongs to me, what I did, could have done, can do."[292] This attitude of responsibility is directly opposed to fatalism which rejects these duties. We are used to thinking that fate and free will are opposites, but free will results in embracing or accepting one's fate. In Jung's words, "Free will is the ability to do gladly that which I must do."[293]

The connection between the Fates and an attitude of thoughtful reflection is woven into their garments. In the *Orphic Hymn to the Fates* they are described as "clothed in purple,"[294] or *kalche*. *Kalchaino* means both "to search for the purple fish," which were the mollusks used to make purple dye, and "to search in the depths of one's mind."[295] Fate desires our awareness, it wants us to search by pondering on the events of our lives. To do this means touching the purple hem of our fate.

In Aeschylus's play "Prometheus Bound," we overhear a chorus of sea nymphs called the Okeanides engaged in conversation with Prometheus, who has seen a bit of his own fate:

> Prometheus: Craft is far weaker than necessity.
> Chorus: Who then is the steersman of necessity?
> Prometheus: The three-formed Fates and the remembering Furies.
> Chorus: And is Zeus, then, weaker than these?
> Prometheus: Yes, for he too cannot escape what is fated.[296]

Craft—that which can be wrought—is far weaker than what is fated. Related to our plans and our designs upon things, craft is what we can do with our two hands. In other words, craft has to do with what we can make happen, requiring willfulness, what can be called our heroic reach. That it is Prometheus who clarifies the difference between craft and fate helps us imagine further into this idea. Prometheus is the Titan who dared circumvent Nature and disrupt the order of the cosmos by stealing fire from Zeus and giving it to mortals. His aim was to elevate humankind with divine knowledge so they could surpass their inherent limitations. Both of these aims reveal Prometheus's *hubris*, the Greek word for excessive pride, that leads to defiance of the gods and his punishment.

Where are we to find these inscrutable goddesses, where lies the map of our fate? Like the unfathomable source of the soul, so the location of the Fates' home cannot be pinpointed. In the Orphic Hymn comes this description: "O many-named dwellers on the lake of heaven where the frozen water by night's warmth is broken inside a sleek cave's shady hollow."[297] The waters that surround their home are fluid and solid at the same time. This suggests fate is both something essential (solid) and perspectival (fluid), and that we find our necessity in the way in which we think about our lives. "Catching the sly winks of fate is a reflective act. It is an act of thought,"[298] advises Hillman. The questions we ask, the pondering, reflecting, feeling, and thinking we engage in, these are the psychic places in between the experiences that become soulful events, between the concrete happening and the symbolic resonance of our life, between frozen ice and warm interior flow. So, whether we engage in the disciplines of astrology and the intricacies of our birth chart, or in psychoanalysis and our complexes, fate is a matter of how we reflect upon what happens in our lives, as well as by asking: how do these things fit? What is the story, the pattern, that is unfolding? In this way experiences become soul events that matter, that have weight and import, that reveal something of our deep nature and necessity. In all of these ways we turn to fate rather than run from it. This pleases these Korai goddesses.

Furies or Erinyes

To live an integral life, we need to pay attention to inner principles, which is to say we must pay homage to our daimon and the gods. By *daimon*, I mean the sense of destiny felt as what we must do in life, who we are, and what we have to have. We can think of this as the personified presence of that which is between fate and character. By *gods*, I mean the deep instinctive forces in us that require our careful attention. Part of paying homage or responding to instincts is to know when to say *no* to one archetypal principle in order to pay appropriate attention to another. This is the human dilemma; we are regularly caught between gods. Being conscious, we could say, means being caught, and consciousness is the therapy of caughtness. The Furies personify the force of whatever life instinct has not been paid attention to and no one can escape their hounding gait.

In Greek they are called *Erinyes*, "Angry or Strong Ones," and their names are Alekto "Unceasing or Never-ending," Tisiphone "Retaliation or Retribution," and Megaira "Grudge or Envious Anger."[299] Ovid describes the Furies as "implacable, doom-laden,"[300] with snakes covering their bodies in tangled clasps that also twine through their white hair. Kerényi says their skin is black and their dresses are grey.[301] Ovid calls them *Sorores Genitae Nocte*, Night-Born Sisters.[302] They are also known as the *Eerophoitis* or Mist Walking, and they carry whips and torches to light their way at night and in Hades.[303]

Revered by all the gods, the Furies are Korai whose powers of retribution are sovereign. In Aeschylus's *Eumenides*, we hear them speak of their divine rights: "Even at birth, I say, our rights were so ordained. The deathless gods must keep their hands off…the Moirai [Fates] who gave us power made us free."[304] Their greatest mandate is to pursue violators of the ancient laws of kinship, which hold sacred the bonds of trust and loyalty within a family. Interfamilial murder or betrayal are their summons, and their terrible reprisal has to do with the consequences of violating fundamental principles of relationship. The Furies thus remind us of the gravity of ancestral and familial ties, and the terrible power at work in the betrayal of those loyalties. These figures reflect the impulse in ourselves, and perhaps in the universe itself, to compensate for treachery.

Like a seed that carries within itself the elements that define what it will become, the birth stories of the gods, who their parents are and the tale of their union, reveal the qualities of consciousness the newborn god brings into the cosmos. The Furies were daughters of the primordial Gaia and Ouranos, Earth and Sky, whose embraces formed the visible world and hundreds of gods and monsters, including the Titans.[305]

Reviling his offspring, Ouranos hid them in secret places within Gaia's expansive body which caused her great pain. With the help of their son Kronos, "the wily, youngest and most terrible,"[306] Gaia devised a plan to free herself and her unborn children. Lying in ambush for the moment when Ouranos reached down for Gaia, Kronos severed Ouranos' genitals from his body with a sickle. The Furies were born from the drops of blood that fell upon the Earth. That Ouranos betrays his children with his repressive hatred, and in turn is betrayed by Gaia and Kronos, suggests that there is a link between violation, betrayal, and the birth of the retributive Furies. Gaia personifies the abundant Earth teeming with life, and when Ouranos suppresses the life that has taken form inside her, he violates the deepest values of her nature. This rupture is what occasions the Furies, as they are the dynamism of vengeance that occurs when the integrity that underlies such alliances are damaged. They spring from Ouranos' blood as defenders of the bonds of relationship.

The Furies are inside the rage of the one who has been betrayed. Hounded, haunted, tormented by the treachery, when we suffer the blow of betrayal we are driven to go over every detail of the deed. This is when we become acquainted with the Furies by their other name, *Maniai*. Bringing a tormented madness to those they stalk, the manic thoughts that accompany betrayal are their song which only the victim of their hunt could hear, a frenzied chant likened to lightning "ripping across the lyre"[307] of the mind. Kerényi says their voice was "like the lowing of cattle; but usually their approach was heralded by a sound of barking,"[308] a sound that also accompanies Hekate, goddess of the underworld and the dark moon. These associations take us to the recesses in the psyche, where bitterness and rage live in lunar shadows.

Hillman writes that betrayal is only possible in relationships where there is primal trust, "Wherever there is trust in a union, the risk of betrayal becomes a real possibility. And betrayal, as a continual possibility to be lived with, belongs to trust as doubt belongs to a living faith."[309] Greek storytellers explored this intimately complicated territory of trust and betrayal in many family dramas, for death at the hands of one's kin is among the sharpest psychological images of this double-sided coin. We read of Althaea who upon hearing that her son Meleager killed her brothers (his uncles) during a hunt on the mountain Calydon, called out to the Furies for justice, "And out of the world of darkness a Fury heard her cries, stalking the night with a Fury's brutal heart."[310] The length of Meleager's life depended on a magic olive branch which Althaea protected, but in her anger at her son for killing her brothers she threw the branch into a fire and Meleager dropped dead. There is also the darkly famed Medea the "murderess" who kills her two young sons in order to take revenge upon Jason, her lover and their father, who left her for another woman.

These mythic family configurations invite the question, *what does it mean to kill a part of your family, that is, an integral part of yourself?* These stories challenge us to reflect on the rage that besets a human heart when something it loves is denied or destroyed. When some blood part of our psyche is refused, the Furies turn up. These issues bring us to reflect on the Kore part of us that is in tune with what is of value, what gives us a sense of individual integrity, what connects us to our ground of being. As the guardians of psychic integrity, the Furies are chthonic forces in league with these deep Kore values.

Another myth where the Furies play a central role is that of Orestes, a tale awash in familial murder and the rippling consequences when a deep principle is offended. Orestes kills his mother Clytemnestra because she murdered her husband and his father, Agamemnon. Agamemnon himself is the progenitor of this bloodsoaked chain of events, for when he sacrificed their daughter Iphigenia in order to set sail to Troy and partake in the great war, Clytemnestra's heart blackened against him. It is Orestes who lives out the impossible tension of this family constellation, and in avenging his father's honor he commits the gravest offense against his mother. The Furies are called forth by Orestes's matricide, and they hunt him despite his coming under Apollo's protection. Killing his mother for killing his father, hunted by the Furies and tenuously shielded by Apollo, Orestes is torn between the gods. He depicts the very human psychological suffering when we are unable to chart a course between their demands.[311] His hardship dramatizes what happens when we give over to one instinct at the cost of another that deserves equal respect. The life lesson here would be that one does not act out these impulses, because in doing so you end up in blind servitude to one god and offending another.

The human challenge is to navigate between the impulses and the deeper principles at work in them, which at times feels impossible. But this is the dilemma of life.

In the Greek tradition, the blood guilt that accompanied any act of murder could only be resolved by a rite of purification and atonement which cleansed the perpetrator of the transgression. In psychological terms, the ritual work shows how whether we are the betrayer or betrayed, we must acknowledge the deed so that it may be properly adjudicated. To atone means to make whole one's experience, to be in integrity with it, *at-one-ment*. Reconciling oneself to the betrayal one has endured, Hillman says, is what may eventually allow for an integration of the experience. This "fidelity to the dark side of the psyche,"[312] carries the possibility of leading to a recognition of the betrayal as having some necessity for the soul, and it is this reconciliation to the event itself that, in due course, can put an end to the hounding feelings of fury.

One of the functions of betrayal is to separate us from our unconscious investment of security and surety in others. We are thrown back on ourselves and wounded, but through the wounding comes consciousness. Perhaps we needed to be shown the blindness of our innocence, or increase our awareness of how power undermines fidelity. As an experience for the deepening of consciousness, betrayal may appear in retrospect to have been necessary in the process of psychological maturity. This is one way to imagine the deeper logic of how the Furies become the Kindly Ones or Eumenides. This metamorphosis occurs through the intervention of Athena who was summoned due to the impasse between claims the Furies and Apollo both made over Orestes. Athena soothes the Furies righteous anger by promising them a place within the walls of the city and confers upon them their new name, the Kindly Ones. That the Furies are made a place within civilized community and become benevolent goddesses suggests metamorphosis is possible. In other words, coming to terms with the necessity of betrayal and other trials of the soul makes integral that which was violent and fracturing. The soul's integrity encompasses both the fury that cleaves and the kindness that soothes.

Pausanias wrote that there were several sanctuaries near Megalopolis in Arkadia where the worshippers offered sacrifice to both the Furies and

Kindly Ones.[313] It is said that when the Furies were pursuing Orestes as he fled from his mother's murder, they were black. He chewed off his finger in torment, which transfigured the goddesses, who then appeared to him as white, and his madness departed. In full knowledge of his crime and in reverence to these powers, he "offered a sin-offering to the black goddesses to avert their wrath, while to the white deities he sacrificed a thank-offering."[314] Orestes makes whole the crime, he atones, by holding side by side the wrongdoing and its reparations.

The Furies are also the avengers of false oaths, covenant-breaking, and perjury. Hesiod says they helped Eris "Strife" give birth to Horcos "Oath."[315] The Furies home is near the river Styx, whose sacred waters are used by the gods in their rituals of oath-swearing. Carried by Iris to Olympus, the water from the Styx bears witness to any oath sworn, and this solemn commitment carries severe punishments for any god if they break their promise, including not being allowed to drink ambrosia for a year as well as a kind of banishment where for the following nine years they are shunned by the other gods. The quality of these waters is precise and unique. They are not the alchemical waters of dissolution, nor are they dewy life-giving waters, rather they are formative, coagulating waters. A binding agent, they are an element of sacred commitment and make witness for the Furies what has been sworn to be true. The waters of Styx come from a source that lies beneath the surface, suggesting that something below our conscious choice registers what has been promised. It's the soul's accounting of our deepest commitments, which when forsworn or betrayed bring forth the Furies from the shores of these very waters, bringing "deep pains of retribution."[316]

Hesiod also says that the Furies track the daily journey of the sun. This conveys how, just as the bonds of relationship are forged by the deeper laws of nature, so too is the world. Guardians of integrity, the Furies' watchful eyes encompass the cosmos as avenging goddesses in service to the deep laws of living a life that honors the fateful bonds we have to the gods. We thus have to wonder just how much our departure from the cosmic rhythms of life prime the Furies.

CHAPTER TWELVE

Sirens

Siren means "entwiner" or "binder," and to these goddesses who are half bird and half maiden belongs the art of seduction. Their voices are unparalleled in beauty, so much so it is said that Thelxiepeia "Enchantress," Agalope "Glorious Voice," and Peisinoe "Affecting the Mind" have charmed the winds with their songs.[317] Daughters of Melpomene, the Muse of tragedy, and the ocean god Achelous, from the rocky perch of their island home they bewitch sailors by awakening in them the desire for divine knowledge. Gifted with prophetic insight, the Sirens' songs promise to tell the truth of things that have come to pass and what is yet to be. Their power takes effect at midday when a windless calm rests upon the ocean waves and everyone is lulled into a waking dream. And upon the lingering notes of their promises of fulfillment comes a swift death.

Odysseus and Jason are among the few who are given the opportunity to hear the Sirens without losing their lives. Odysseus owes his safe passage to Circe who warns how these goddesses will endeavor to lure his crew to their death, a danger they must risk in order to journey home. But how can curious Odysseus resist hearing their devastating song? Cleverly, he devises a plan and has the crew stuff wax into their ears while he is lashed to the mast so that he may listen without risk of falling under their spell and overpowering his crew to their death. Odysseus allows us too to hear what they promise:

> Odysseus! Come here! You are well-known
> From many stories! Glory of the Greeks!
> Now stop your ship and listen to our voices.
> All those who pass this way hear honeyed song,
> poured from our mouths. The music brings them joy,
> and they go on their way with greater knowledge,
> since we know everything the Greeks and Trojans
> suffered in Troy, by gods' will; and we know
> whatever happens anywhere on earth.[318]

The Sirens' song appeals not to the desire of the body, but the desire of the spirit that wants to transcend its human limitations. Promising knowledge of all that will come to pass, how can we doubt their urgent honeyed words do not stir the hero's desire? "It is strange and beautiful," writes Jane Ellen Harrison, "that Homer should make the Sirens appeal to the spirit, not to the flesh. To primitive man, Greek or Semite, the desire to know—to be as the gods—was the fatal desire."[319] Heroic consciousness experiences the Sirens as devourers because the greatest temptation for the hero is to strive *to know* as the gods. This danger is ubiquitous because hubris, the blind spot of ego consciousness, is a part of the human condition. *There is more that can be known,* call out the Sirens, thereby awakening us to those parts that are full of imperious longings for that which lies beyond our ken. Personifying this seductive call of the spirit, they show how integral to our human nature it is to try to reach beyond ourselves.

The *sirenum scopuli* or corpse-littered waters that demarcate their islands attest to how dangerous it is to listen to their song from the heroic-ego attitude. Like Phaeton trying to steer the chariot of the Sun without proper skill or strength, the call that inspires us to go beyond our limits can be fatal if responded to without restraint. Unconsciously identifying with the gods is psychologically destructive, and believing oneself to be the Great Mother who must care for everyone, or Aphrodite incarnate, we lose our ego-bound sense of self and can quite literally go mad. Being practiced in the art of self-binding like Odysseus is a necessary skill as it is restraint that protects one from being devoured by the Sirens, who will ravish you to dissolution.

While they are most well known for their rapturous death song, it is only one aspect of their myth. Depending on where you stand and the kind of listening that stance invites, the Siren's song offers something else entirely. Circe's instructions to Odysseus makes this clear, "If anyone goes near them in ignorance, and listens to their voices, that man will never travel home."[320] "In ignorance" is key. To tune into their song with heroic hubris is to perish, whereas to listen with awareness of limitation, and with an understanding of what is at stake, we might hear what elevates the soul.

An earlier chapter of the goddesses' lives shows us one such stance. They were once Kore with fair and fully human bodies. Ovid says they were gathering flowers with Persephone on the day she disappeared, and when they heard Demeter cry out that her daughter was lost, they went to search but were unable to find her no matter how far they ran.[321] In distress, they wove their voices into a plea and beseeched the gods to be given wings so they could move farther, see further and "glide over the sea."[322] The gods granted them their wish, and golden wings replaced their fair arms, golden feathers covered their breasts, and talons replaced their toes. So not to lose their mesmerizing gift of poetry and song, the gods left their beautiful faces and human voices unchanged.

The Sirens sang so that Persephone could hear their voices and find her way to them. I take this to mean that Kore consciousness can experience the Siren's songs as north stars, calling us to move beyond our limited perspective and gain further knowledge of ourselves and the world. In the promise of that expansion, sometimes we're fated to hear their song and so be transported beyond our small world. In my own life, this was very much the case. I grew up in New York City in the 1980s, when it was truly a melting pot of nationalities. My mother immigrated alone from Czechoslovakia and my father, half Italian and half Dominican, was a first generation American. Though no one in my immediate family had been to college, it was my dream to do so. Higher education was not part of the family story, yet I heard this call to reach for something that was not on the map of the world I knew. I now understand the feelings and im-

185

Ssdrov

pulses around college and, later, graduate school to have been the Siren's melody that awakened in me a desire to step into the world and develop a bigger view. At the same time this was one of my early initiations into korehood. Reflecting on it now, I would say I navigated the dangers of the expansive horizons by always staying close to what mattered, which is to be in service to big, beautiful ideas. The desire for a life of scholarship rendered clear the necessary commitments, disciplines, and devotions, and it was these that formed my ship-mast, the restraints that kept me safe in uncharted waters. This clarity of vocation is one of the greatest blessings in my life, and it has carried me through difficult times. It is as if the presence of the Kore and sense of daimonic purpose allow a person to hear the song of the Siren's without being carried away.

Graiai

The Graiai are called well-clad Pemphredo "She Who Shows the Way," "Warlike" Enyo in saffron robes, and Deino the "Terrible."[323] Sisters and secret keepers of the Gorgons, they are the daughters of the water serpent Phorcys and Keto or "She Who Breaches." Ancient water ways are born upon the body of deep swirling Keto, a Titan goddess of the sea whose name is connected to *ketea*, the feminine form of "sea monster."[324] Her daughters, the Graiai and Sirens, give us a sense of her primeval creativity and power. These island-dwelling Korai come from Keto's oceanic womb, their bodies like waves that peak and crest upon the infinite sea.

Graia means old woman, for though the Graiai were born youthful and "fair cheeked," they had grey hair.[325] Hair is expressive of the quality of one's spirit and state of mind. An abundance of hair bespeaks potency, while unbound and flowing it evokes freedom and desire. Unloosened hair is associated with grief and mourning, and shorn hair a sign of willing sacrifice. Grey hair generally comes with age and is related to maturity, authority, and experience—the Graiai came into the world wise.

A mixture of black and white, grey mediates between these two primary shades and softens the contrasts. In these places where permeable areas are preferred over clean lines, like watercolors flowing into one another, delicate intricacies and variation are invited in. Shades of grey connote the nuances of life, which is conveyed in the phrase "it's a grey area" to suggest a lack of clear rules or understanding. Graiai-grey is a quality exuded by moist air: as clouds that soften the border between sky and land, early morning mists rising from a forest floor, or a descending fog that obscures the lines of a landscape. The Graiai bring an awareness of the ambiguity that lies beyond the known, occupying the grey places in-between. This aspect of Kore consciousness is concerned with the softer liminal place between black and white where paradoxes are permitted. Far from lacking color, grey bespeaks a potent psychological field where both/and awareness makes room for possibilities and flow.

This Graiai-grey quality of consciousness is discernible in every feature of their mythos. Their island home is called Kisthene, the land of rock roses, located far along the edge of Okeanos.[326] There, it is said, neither the sun nor the moon shines and so they live in perpetual twilight, that mediating period of time that hovers on the edge between night and day. Twilight is the softest imaginable border between light and darkness. This is an edge beloved of Tess, the protagonist in *Tess of the d'Urbervilles,* who "knew how to hit to a hair's-breadth that moment of evening when the light and the darkness are so evenly balanced that the constraint of day and the suspense of night neutralize each other, leaving absolute mental liberty. It is then that the plight of being alive becomes attenuated to its least possible dimensions."[327] Tess touches freedom in the in-between of the gloaming, a moment where one seems outside the time-bounded order that encircles our days.

In addition to their swanlike grey hair and their twilight home, the Graiai have only one eye and one tooth among them. They must circulate the sense means of seeing, tasting, and savoring. Sharing the organs of knowledge, their knowing has a communal quality. Their eyesight is circulated in a peculiar dance between insight as a looking in and vision as a seeing out, their outstretched hands continually giving and receiving. Enyo takes the eye and passes to Pemphredo the tooth, all six hands holding the eye that gives sight to each.

CHAPTER THIRTEEN

Sibling Archetype and the Kore

The Korai triad goddesses present constellations of the psyche in multiple configurations—the Graiai with their one eye and tooth, and the Furies who shape-shift into the Kindly Ones. While they have individual names, and like the Hours may even have stories that feature one or another of them, we mostly do not know these goddesses apart from their sisterhood. Thus we are faced with this paradox—the Kore is unto-herself and yet the larger archetypal sibling configuration helps us further grasp korehood.

While the triad goddesses show how the Kore archetype expresses itself in multiplicity, individuality is this pattern's most prominent quality. The Kore is about reinforcing one's own unique stance and being connected to the ground of one's values. There are many ways in which we discover ourselves, but it is in sibling relationships that individuality is instinctively learned, because they create the very conditions that necessitate differentiation. As such, sibling ties are of great importance in terms of our individual psychological experience and thus are intrinsic to the life of the soul. Here, I think, lies the essence of the paradoxical expressions of Kore multiplicity.

In *The Sibling Archetype*, Gustavo Barcellos elucidates the profundity of siblinghood, noting it is "primarily with brothers and sisters that we brothers / sisters /

learn the difficult lessons of horizontality, continuity, symmetrical relations, and soul-making."[328] Developing a sense of one's general position
is easy in relationships that are hierarchical. With parents and parental
figures this *verticality* is made clear by age, authority and distinct levels
of responsibility. With siblings differentiation and identity is of another
order because, generally speaking, siblings are of the same generation,
occupying similar positions hierarchically, and therefore equal regardless
who was born first or last. Siblings thus inhabit a *horizontality* where
the exchange between self and other is essentially nonhierarchical. As
Barcellos observes, the sibling archetype is characterized by "horizontal
symmetric styles of consciousness"[329] and relating on a plane of equality
and difference. Thus it is with siblings where we learn about, "deepening
in the horizontal place, toward the Other, the world and its events and
complications."[330] Archetypal horizontality then is a direction of growth
in conscious individuality.

At the same time that one learns how to relate to another, sibling
bonds also pose a fundamental question regarding one's own identity—
how do you become the individual you are in relation to your siblings
and then later on in relationships with friends and peers? This concern,
which belongs to the Kore, is brought into consciousness through those
primary kinship ties where issues of sameness and difference are worked.
Whether or not we have siblings, we require sibling-style bonds wherein
we discover ourselves in both connection and contrast to someone like
us. This has to do with how a sense of self is born through relating with
others. Whether our siblings are real, surrogate or even imaginal, there
is a part of us that needs an other to mirror back to us who we are and
who we are not. For women, it is with those we regard as sisters that
we often work out and face our deepest desires, our fears, who we have
been, who we are, and who we are becoming. Sisterhood is thus about
finding individuality and community, which speaks to the intensity and
sometimes alienating potential of these configurations.

Within the sibling archetypal field move the skillful hands of the Fates,
for the psychological task of distinguishing oneself is embedded in what
we mean by fate. The unique person we are, that sense of a particular life
and vision which we must live into, all contribute to a sense of necessity,

which overlaps with a sense of calling. Is not our sense of fate one of the ways that we distinguish ourselves from our siblings and our peers?

Christine Downing enters the terrain of sisterhood through the stories of mortal sisters in Greek myth to explore the complex nature of sister-sister relationships in women's experience. As she illuminates in the myth of Psyche, whose sisters are compelled by a poisonous envy to attempt the destruction of her life, or the painful separation of Antigone and Ismene who cannot see eye to eye over issues of family honor, everything from envy, competitiveness, unquestioning love, and the pains of distance are all part of what arises in the sister-sister dyad. Looking at how the sister archetype gives depth and meaning to the development of one's identity Downing writes, "Like ourselves…the mortal women of Greek mythology become themselves through engagement with others, through projection, differentiation, and reintegration, through struggle and suffering, love and hatred, failure and death."[331] With sisters we make conscious aspects of ourselves through the inexplicably near other.

The archetypal pattern of the sibling also helps create differentiation in terms of the relational dynamics we encounter in life. Most significantly, sibling consciousness helps us move out of the parent/child configuration, a hierarchically structured connection defined by a mix of love and power. For Barcellos, and for Hillman too, to see by means of the sibling archetype would mean questioning the parental focus that has dominated psychological ideas. From the parental lens, the view of the psyche is a developmental one characterized by progression and verticality; the life of the soul is imagined in terms of growth and maturity. All roads lead back to Mother and Father. Through this lens, korehood is seen as a transitional phase on the way to motherhood, for the virgin-daughter is meant to become a mother. In contrast, a psychology that sees by means of the sibling archetype brings to the foreground issues of individuality, diversity and equality.

The way sibling consciousness sees equality despite differences is profoundly important in terms of larger social life. Sisterhood has always been the way women have characterized their endeavors to raise consciousness on women's issues. In its most far reaching and inclusive form, being a feminist can be defined as a belief in women having equal rights and opportunities—legally, financially, politically, medically, religiously, institutionally, professionally—and the fundamental right to choose how to tend their physical well-being. All women belong under this wide umbrella, which is constructed by an intersectional frame, no matter one's race, color, economic status, health concerns or political persuasions. In it's ideal form, feminist sisterhood combines the possibilities of discovering and maintaining one's individuality while relating to others with a sense of belonging and responsibility. These principles of equality is what the Furies protect, for they personify the understanding that there are a certain set of guidelines by which people need to live, otherwise the community breaks down. The archetypal ideal of sisterhood is an inclusivity that honors difference.

As important as horizontal deepening is, sibling consciousness is not solely an outward posture. The sibling metaphor and its intimacies offer an inward facing, interiorizing movement related to the banding of soul figures that comprise our personality. In other words, inner sisterhood is what grows out of our paying attention to our psyche. The Kore's unto-one-self nature is ultimately an interior perspective where going 'in' means staying close to the figures of the psyche. In dialogue with these imaginal presences, as I reflect on an issue, my self-understanding is a gathering of perspectives. There are a number of ways by which I can consider a matter, as if the 'me' that is 'I' is accompanied by other persons of my soul—the hungry child, the fierce hunter, the reclusive crone. The Korai triads bespeak an intimate internal multiplicity, generating the 'withness' Jungian analyst Edward Edinger describes as the relational factor of consciousness itself: "The process of becoming conscious requires both seeing and being seen, knowing and being known."[332] At the root of consciousness is a *being with* that is characterized by movement, flow, exchange, and circulation. This sense of accompaniment is the eros connection consciousness requires. The Graces clasp hands and begin dancing with Aphrodite, flowers blossoming under their feet with each step. As sister figures of deep interiority, the Korai triads personify the relationship that develops when we are in connection to the figures of our inner world.

Inner sisterhood is akin to what Jung called the "inner friend of the soul," which he discussed in relation to the dream motif wherein an individual is reborn into another person: "This 'other being' is the other person in ourselves—that larger and greater personality maturing within us."[333] The development of this other personality is central to the individuation process. Amplifying this through mythic images that depict friendship, he continues, "it reveals our relationship to that inner friend of the soul into whom Nature herself would like to change us—that other person who we are also and yet can never attain to completely. We are that pair of Dioscuri, one of whom is mortal and the other immortal, and who, though always together, can never be made completely one."[334]

Yet this "inner friend" might also be imagined as the presence of inner *friendship*. For many women who engage korehood, the Self seems to appear in just this way. The Self wants to remind us of our totality and our roots in something greater, deeper and finally, more cosmological, which has to be consciously grappled with, for not to wrestle with Nature is to remain unconscious. Inner friendship grows out of attention given to each part. The qualities of sovereignty, integrity, individuality and vitality that the Kore personifies reflect the indivisible poise that comes from being a witness to inner division. Just as mythic mortal sisters can move us towards exploring the significance of our relationships with other women, the Korai move us inward into a sisterhood with the psyche and the Self. Jung's "colloquy with the friend of the soul"[335] can be imagined as a conversation with soul sisters.

APPENDIX

Kore Studies

This selected list highlights creative works wherein the Kore archetype is afoot, and which have been most instructive and inspiring in my study of this figure.

NOVELS

Anne of Green Gables (1908), L. M. Montgomery
Cassandra (1983), Christa Wolf
Dragonfly Sea (2019), Yvonne Adhiambo Owuor
Neapolitan Quartet (2012-2015), Elena Ferrante
The Elegance of the Hedgehog (2006), Muriel Barbery
The Forsythe Saga (1922), John Galsworthy
The Mists of Avalon (1982), Marion Zimmer Bradley
Wicked (1995), Gregory Maguire

FILMS

Auntie Mame (1958), directed by Morton DaCosta
Crouching Tiger, Hidden Dragon (2000), directed by Ang Lee

Mad Max: Fury Road (2015), directed by George Miller
Mustang (2015), directed by Deniz Gamze Ergüven
Portrait of a Lady on Fire (2019), directed by Céline Sciamma
Thelma and Louise (1991), directed by Ridley Scott
Virgin Suicides (2000), directed by Sofia Coppola
Whale Rider (2003), directed by Niki Caro

TELEVISION

The Golden Girls (1985–1992), created by Susan Harris

NOTES

INTRODUCTION

1. Le Guin, 1989, p. 4
2. Paris, 1986, p. 3
3. Hillman, 2004, p. 31
4. Cornford, 1923, p. 69
5. Cashford, 1998, p. 117
6. Paris, 1986, p. 114
7. Paris, 1986, p. 114
8. Hall, 1980, p. 68
9. Jung, 1969, p. 87 *CW* 9 pt. II para. 142
10. Paris, 1986, p.197

CHAPTER ONE

11. Kerényi, 1980, p. 39
12. Jung, 1951/1969, p. 182 *CW* 9 pt. 1 para. 306
13. Jung, 1951/1969, p. 183 *CW* 9 pt. 1 para. 309
14. Originally published as a monograph *Das gottliche Madchen* with Kerényi in 1941 and republished that same year in *Essays on a Science of Mythology*. The revised 1951 version in *CW* 9 pt. 1.
15. Jung, 1951/1969, p. 187 *CW* 9 pt. 1 para. 315
16. Jaffé, 1984, p. 81
17. Jung, 1951/1969, p. 184 *CW* 9 pt. 1 para. 311
18. Jung, 1951/1969, p. 186 *CW* 9 pt. 1 para. 313
19. Jung, 1997, p. 729
20. Agamben and Ferrando, 2014, p. 6
21. Thomas, 2017
22. Aeschylus, 2006, p. 788
23. Harding, 1935, p. 78
24. Jung, 1954/1969, p. 213 *CW* 8 para. 417
25. Jung, 1951/1969, p. 179 *CW* 9 pt. 1 para. 301

26. Harding, 1935, p. 82
27. Harding, 1935, p. 266
28. Harding, 1935, p. 266
29. Harding, 1935, p. vii
30. Harding, 1935, p.102
31. Harding, 1935, p. 106
32. Hollister Wheelwright, 1984, p. 36

33. Hollister Wheelwright, 1984, p. 3
34. Hollister Wheelwright, 1984, p. 23
35. Hollister Wheelwright, 1984, p. 28
36. Claremont de Castillejo, 1997, p. 170
37. Claremont de Castillejo, 1997, p. 167
38. Claremont de Castillejo, 1997, p. 167
39. Claremont de Castillejo, 1997, p. 179

CHAPTER TWO

40. Otto, 1954, p. 7
41. Jones, 2010, p. 92
42. Richter, 1968, p. 1
43. Aubuchon, 2013, p. 1
44. Richter, 1968, p. 3
45. Hurwit, 1999, p. 126
46. Stieber, 2004, pp.1-12
47. Stieber, 2004
48. Richter, 1968
49. Stieber, 2004

50. Richter, 1968, p. 21
51. Karakasi, 2003, plates 236, 237, 245, 248
52. Richter, 1968, pp. 6-20; Stieber 2004, pp. 68-76
53. Richter, 1968, p. 4
54. Stieber, 2004, p. 119
55. Ridgway, 1990
56. Richter, 1968, p. 3

CHAPTER THREE

57. Stieber, 2010, p. 119
58. Stieber, 2010, p. 119
59. O'Keeffe, 1996, p. 11
60. Belk, 2003, p. 6
61. Belk, 2003, p. 4
62. Statista, 2020
63. Belk, 2003, p. 10-11
64. Belk, 2003, p. 10-11
65. Belk, 2003, p. 13
66. Frey et al., 1993
67. Cleary, 1996
68. Cleary, 1996, p. xxi
69. Pinkola Estés, 1992, p. 222
70. Leonard, 1982, p. 11
71. Ferrante, 2012, p. 118

72. Leonard, 1982, p. 17
73. Leonard, 1982, p. 10
74. Ferrante, 2012, p. 248
75. Woodman and Schiwy, 2011, disc 5
76. Guggenheim, 2015
77. Yousafzai, 2014, p. 311
78. Woodman and Dickson, 1997, p. 8
79. von Franz, 1972, p. 97
80. Woodman, 1985, p. 78
81. Angelou, 2009, p. 31
82. Angelou, 2009, p. 32
83. Jung and Kerényi, 1969, p. 106
84. Mylonas, 1961, p. 100
85. Pausanias, I, xxxviii, 3
86. Kerényi, 1991, p. 94

87. Agamben and Ferrando, 2014, p. 55
88. Kerényi, 1991, p. 28
89. Farnell, 1896, vol. 3
90. Downing, 2001, p. 11

91. Jung and Kerényi, 1969, p. 106
92. Smith, 2008, p. 197
93. Kerényi, 1991, p. 44

CHAPTER FOUR

94. Sissa, 1990, p. 77
95. Hall, 1980, p. 11
96. Woodman, 1985, p. 80
97. Woodman, 1985, p. 81
98. Shaw, 2014, p. 9
99. Johnson, 1976, p. 44
100. Farnell, 1896, p. 363
101. Liddell, 1925, I:698
102. Paris, 1986, p. 175
103. Demetrakopolous, 1979, p. 63-4
104. Demetrakopolous, 1979, p. 61
105. Demetrakopolous, 1979, p. 61
106. Hesse, 1971, p. 71
107. Hillman, 2007, p. 235
108. Demetrakopolous, 1979, p. 60
109. Paris, 1986, p.134
110. Boer, 1996, p. 138
111. Otto, 1954, p. 55
112. Irigaray, 1993, p. 110
113. Jung and Kerényi, 1969, p. 104
114. Hall, 1980, p. 98
115. Turner, 2011, p. 20
116. Flori, 2008, p. 18
117. Flori, 2008, p. 19
118. Flori, 2008, p. 238
119. Flori, 2008, p. 4
120. Flori, 2008, p. 26
121. Flori, 2008, p. 43
122. Ulanov, 1971, p. 205
123. Flori, 2008, p. 238
124. Weir, 2001, p. 283
125. Wheeler and Brown, 2008, p. 4

126. Bellonci, 2003, p. 20
127. Bellonci, 2003, p. 21
128. Bellonci, 2003, p. 78
129. Bellonci, 2003, p. 81
130. Bellonci, 2003, p. 99
131. Bradford, 2004, p. 93
132. Bradford, 2004, p. 110
133. Bellonci, 2003, p. 196
134. Bellonci, 2003, p. 229
135. Bradford, 2004, p. 186
136. Bradford, 2004, p. 197
137. Bradford, 2004, p. 145
138. Berry, 2008, p. 93
139. Jung, 1936/1968, p. 159 *CW* 12 para. 208
140. Tait, 2010, 178
141. Hillman, 1997, p. 104
142. Kingsford and Maitland, 1885/2008, p. 23
143. Yeats, 1994, p. 221
144. Irigaray, 1993, p. 117
145. Jung, 1997, p. 757
146. Paris, 1986, p. 109
147. Otto, 1954, p. 83
148. Paris, 1986, p. 110
149. Farnell, 1896/2010, p. 432
150. Farnell, 1896/2010, p. 520. Also Richter, 1968, p. 26
151. Paris, 1986, p. 137
152. Kerényi, 1979, p. 11
153. Ovid, 1993, 4.770
154. Hillman, 1997, p. 208

CHAPTER FIVE

155. Kerényi quoted in Downing, 2000, p. 109
156. Farnell, 2010, v 2 p. 445
157. Mishan, 2020
158. Montgomery, 1982, p. 64
159. Paris, 1986, p. 152
160. Kerényi, 1980, p. 44
161. Amos and Powers, 2005, p. 35
162. Amos and Powers, 2005, p. 35
163. Amos and Powers, 2005, p. 36
164. Amos and Powers, 2005, p. 12
165. Amos and Powers, 2005, p. 13
166. Moore, 1982, p. 54
167. Montgomery, 1982, p. 176
168. Browning quoted in Montgomery, 1982

CHAPTER SIX

169. Jung, 1952/1967, p. 297 *CW* 5 para. 456
170. Jung, 1952/1967, p. 297 *CW* 5 para. 456
171. Hillman, 1996, p. 68
172. Herman, 1989, p. xi
173. Apuleius, 1979, p. 264
174. Gimbutas, 1991
175. Gimbutas, 1989, p. xv
176. Gimbutas, 1989, p. x
177. Gimbutas, 1991, p. 222 and p. 316
178. Gimbutas, 1989
179. Jung, 1954/1968, p. 82 *CW* 9 pt. 1 para. 158
180. Hillman, 1975, p. 51
181. Hillman, 1975, p. 46
182. Campbell, 2013, p. 9
183. Neumann, 1974, p. 47
184. Campbell, 2013, p.32
185. Jung, 1954/1968, p. 81 *CW* 9 pt. 1 para. 156
186. Jung, 1954/1968, p. 82 *CW* 9 pt. 1 para. 158
187. Neumann, 1974, p. 25
188. Neumann, 1974, p. 62
189. Neumann 1974, p. 319
190. Zuntz, 1971, p. 80
191. Zuntz, 1971, p. 77
192. Baring and Cashford, 1993, p. xi
193. Baring and Cashford, 1993, p. xi
194. Kinsley, 1988, p. x
195. Neumann, 1974, p. 6
196. Jung, 1940/1969, p. 49 *CW* 11, para. 87
197. Hillman, 1979, p. 216
198. Neumann, 1974, p. 48

CHAPTER SEVEN

199. Szalai, 2015
200. Macko and Rubin, 2005, loc. 112
201. Levy, 2018, p. xi
202. Hillman, 1979, p. 69
203. Levy, 2018, p. 90
204. Harding, 1935, p. 267

205. Steinem quoted in Orenstein, 2001, p. 127
206. Rich, 2018, p. 154
207. Barbery, 2008, p. 40

208. Jung, 1954/1968, p. 92 *CW* 9 pt. 1 para. 172
209. Herman, 1989, p. 62
210. Orenstein, 2001, p. 284

CHAPTER EIGHT

211. Works that treat the Mother-Daughter mysteries of this myth include Nor Hall's *The Moon and the Virgin*, Maureen Murdock's *The Heroine's Journey*, Kathie Carlson's *Life's Daughter/Death's Bride*, and *The Long Journey Home* edited by Christine Downing.
212. Hillman, "The Great Mother, Her Son, Her Hero, and the Puer" in *Senex and Puer*
213. Aeschylus, 1979, p. 264
214. Wiktionary, 2020
215. Zuntz, 1971, p. 71
216. Carlson, 1997, p. 233, footnote 21
217. Herman, 1989, p. xiv, p. xvii
218. Herman, 1989, p. xiv
219. Boer, 1996, p. 117
220. Herman, 1989, p. 60

221. Neumann, 1974, p. 31
222. Rayor, 2014, p. 28
223. Woodman, 1982, p. 121
224. Woodman, 1982, p. 149
225. Woodman, 1982, p. 148
226. Hillman, 1975, pp. 205-210
227. Herman, 1989, p. 65
228. Woodman and Dickson, 1997, p. 26
229. Hillman, 1997, p. 47
230. Woodman, 1982, p. 67
231. Herman, 1989, p. 55
232. Woodman, 1982, p. 69
233. Jung, 1951/1969, p. 183 *CW* 9 pt. 1 para. 310
234. Jung, 1951/1969, p. 188 *CW* 9 pt. 1 para. 316
235. Rilke, 1990
236. Hollister Wheelwright, 1984, p. 36

CHAPTER NINE

237. The exceptions are exceedingly rare when it comes to the triad goddesses of this study. Harrison makes the observation that the reverse is the case in Late Roman Art. (1991, p. 288-89)
238. See Harrison, 1991; Kerényi, 1969; Wind 1969

239. Hillman, 1975, p. 157
240. Gimbutas, 1989, p. 97
241. Wind, 1969, p. 21

CHAPTER TEN

242. MacLachlan, 1993, p. 4
243. Pindar, 1972, Ode 14
244. Kerényi, 1980, p. 99
245. Milani, 2013, p. 89
246. Pindar, 1972, Ode 14
247. MacLachlan, 1993, p. 4
248. Hillman, 2008, p. 62
249. Boer, 1996, p. 61
250. Hesiod, 1914, p. 145
251. Milani, 2013, p. 90
252. Otto cited in Milani, 2013, p. 80
253. Plato cited in Milani, 2013, p. 9
254. Hillman, 2008, p. 30-32
255. Milani, 2013, p. ix
256. Farnell, 2010, p. 428
257. Harrison, 1991, p. 286
258. Kerényi, 1980, p. 100
259. Kerényi, 1980, p. 100
260. Hillman, 1997, p. xvi
261. Kerényi, 1999, p. 77
262. Salzberg quoted in Tippett, 2016

263. Cohen, Anthem song
264. Harrison, 2010, p. 514f; Kerényi, 1980, p. 101
265. Kerényi, 1980, p. 102
266. Chase Greene, 1968, p. 13
267. Hillman, 2008, p. 47
268. Kerényi, 1980, p. 102
269. Pindar, 1997, 13 str1-ant1
270. Hesiod, 1914, p. 97
271. Ovid, 1993, p. 147
272. Solon, 1999, Fragment 4
273. Ovid, 1931, 1.700
274. Jung, 1929/1967, p. 37 *CW* 13 para. 54
275. Hillman in Heraclitus 2001, p. xvii
276. Evelyn-White, 1914, line 550
277. Sissa, 1990, p. 4
278. Woodman, 1985, p. 81
279. Sissa, 1990, p. 36
280. Sissa, 1990, p. 36
281. Sissa, 1990, p. 37

CHAPTER ELEVEN

282. Hesiod, 1914, p. 258
283. Hesiod, 1914
284. Plato, 1996
285. Hillman, 1996, p. 208
286. Greene, 1984, p. 2
287. Greene, 1984, p. 6
288. Greene, 1984, p. 3
289. Renault, 1988, p. 16
290. Hillman, 1996, p. 251
291. Hillman, 1996, p. 251
292. Hillman, 1996, p. 194
293. Greene and Sasportas, 1988, p. 27
294. Athanassakis, 2013, p. 79

295. Sanford, 2015, p. 1
296. Aeschylus, 2006, p. 513
297. Athanassakis, 2013, p. 2
298. Hillman, 1996, p. 194
299. Harrison, 1991, p. 214
300. Ovid, 1993, 4.454
301. Kerényi, 1980, p. 48
302. Ovid, 1993, 4.454
303. Homer, 1990, 19.85
304. Aeschylus, 1984, line 350
305. Hesiod, 1914, p. 93
306. Hesiod, 1914, p. 89
307. Aeschylus, 1984, line 331

308. Kerényi, 1980, p. 47

309. Hillman, 2005, p. 196

310. Homer, 1990, p. 698

311. See Hillman, "Athena, Ananke and Abnormal Psychology" in *Mythic Figures*

312. Hillman, 2005, p. 212

313. Pausanias, 1984, 8.34.1

314. Pausanias, 1984, 8.34.1

315. Hesiod, 1914, p. 63

316. Athanassakis, 2013, p. 69

CHAPTER TWELVE

317. Hesiod, 1914, p. 181

318. Homer, 2018, p. 307

319. Harrison, 1991, p. 198

320. Homer, 2018, p. 302

321. Ovid, 1993, p. 169

322. Ovid, 1993, p. 169

323. Hesiod, 1914, p. 99

324. Kerényi, 1980, p. 34

325. Kerényi, 1980, p. 45

326. Kerényi, 1980, p. 46

327. Hardy, 2003, p. 85

CHAPTER THIRTEEN

328. Barcellos, 2016, p. 54

329. Barcellos, 2016, p. 54

330. Barcellos, 2016, p. 54

331. Downing, 1988, p. 16

332. Edinger, 1984, p. 53

333. Jung, 1950/1968, p. 131 *CW* 9 pt. 1 para. 235

334. Jung, 1950/1968, p. 131 *CW* 9 pt. 1 para. 235

335. Jung, 1950/1968, p. 131 *CW* 9 pt. 1 para. 235

BIBLIOGRAPHY

Aeschylus. (1979). *The Oresteia*. (Robert Fagles, Trans.). Penguin Classics.

Aeschylus. (2006). *Aeschylus: Suppliant maidens. Persians. Prometheus. Seven against Thebes*. Reprint ed. Loeb Classical Library.

Agamben, Giorgio, and Monica Ferrando. (2014). *The unspeakable girl: The myth and mystery of Kore*. Seagull Books.

Amos, Tori. (1994). Take to the sky. On *Under the pink* [CD]. Atlantic Records.

Amos, Tori, and Ann Powers. (2005). *Tori Amos: Piece by piece*. Broadway.

Angelou, Maya, and Oprah Winfrey. (2009). *I know why the caged bird sings*. Reissue ed. Ballantine Books.

Apuleius. (1979). *The golden ass: The transformations of Lucius*. Farrar, Straus and Giroux.

Athanassakis, Apostolos N. (Trans.) (2013). *The Orphic hymns*. Johns Hopkins University Press.

Aubuchon, Rachel. (2013). *Individuality and anonymity in archaic Greek sculpture: Questions of form in the kore type* (Publication No. 1538009) [Master's thesis, University of North Carolina at Chapel Hill]. ProQuest Dissertations and Theses Global.

Barbery, Muriel. (2008). *The elegance of the hedgehog*. Europa Editions.

Barcellos, Gustavo. (2016). *The sibling archetype: The psychology of brothers and sisters and the meaning of horizontality*. Spring Publications.

Baring, Anne, and Jules Cashford. (1993). *The myth of the goddess: Evolution of an image.* Penguin.

Belk, Russell W. (2003). Shoes and Self. *Advances in consumer research* 30, 27–33.

Bellonci, Maria. (2003). *The life and times of Lucrezia Borgia.* Phoenix.

Berry, Patricia. (2008). *Echo's subtle body: Contributions to an archetypal psychology.* 2nd ed. Spring Publications.

Boer, Charles. (Trans.). (1996). *The Homeric hymns.* 2nd ed. Spring Publications.

Bradford, Sarah. (2004). *Lucrezia Borgia: Life, love and death in renaissance Italy.* Viking.

Burkert, Walter. (1985). *Greek religion.* Reprint edition. Harvard University Press.

Campbell, Joseph. (2013). *Goddesses: Mysteries of the feminine divine.* (S. Rossi, Ed.). New World Library.

Carlson, Kathie. (1997). *Life's daughter/death's bride.* Shambhala.

Cashford, Jules. (1998). Reflecting Mirrors: Ideas of Personal and Archetypal Gender. *Harvest* 44(2), 105–18.

Claremont de Castillejo, Irene. (1997). *Knowing woman: A feminine psychology.* Revised ed. Shambhala.

Cleary, Thomas. (1996). *Immortal sisters: Secret teachings of Taoist women.* North Atlantic Books.

Cohen, Leonard. (1992). Anthem song. On *The Future* [CD]. Columbia Records.

Cornford, Francis Macdonald. (1923). *Greek religious thought from Homer to the age of Alexander.* J.M. Dent & Son.

Demetrakopolous, Stephanie A. (1979). Hestia, goddess of the hearth: notes on an oppressed archetype. *Spring: An Annual of Archetypal Psychology and Jungian Thought:* 55–75.

Douglas, Claire. (1989). *The woman in the mirror: analytical psychology and the feminine.* Sigo Press.

Downing, Christine. (1988). *Psyche's sisters: Reimagining the meaning of sisterhood.* Harper & Row.

——(2000). *The goddess: mythological images of the feminine.* Continuum.

——(Ed.). (2001). *The long journey home: Revisioning the myth of Demeter and Persephone for our time.* Shambhala.

Edinger, Edward F. (1984). *The creation of consciousness: Jung's myth for modern man.* Inner City Books.

Estés, Clarissa Pinkola. (1992). *Women who run with the wolves: Myths and stories of the wild woman archetype.* Ballantine Books.

Farnell, Lewis Richard. (1896). *The cults of the Greek states.* Cambridge University Press.

Ferrante, Elena. (2012). *My brilliant friend: Neapolitan novels, book one*. Penguin.

Flori, Jean. (2008). *Eleanor of Aquitaine: Queen and rebel*. Edinburgh University Press.

Frey, C., Thompson, F., Smith, J., Sanders, M., & Horstman, H. (1993). American Orthopaedic Foot and Ankle Society women's shoe survey. *Foot & ankle*, 14(2), 78–81.

Gimbutas, Marija. (1989). *The language of the goddess: Unearthing the hidden symbols of Western civilization*. Harper & Row.

——(1991). *The civilization of the goddess: The world of old Europe*. (J. Marler, Ed.). HarperCollins.

Greene, Liz. (1984). *The astrology of fate*. Weiser Books.

Greene, Liz, and Howard Sasportas. (1988). *Dynamics of the unconscious: seminars in psychological astrology*. Weiser Books.

Greene, William Chase. (1968). *Moira: Fate, good, and evil in Greek thought*. 2nd ed. P. Smith.

Guggenheim, Davis. (2015). *He named me Malala*. Fox Searchlight.

Hall, Nor. (1980). *The moon and the virgin*. Harper & Row.

Harding, Esther. (1935). *Woman's mysteries: Ancient & modern*. Longmans, Green and Co.

Hardy, Thomas. (2003). *Tess of the D'Urbervilles*. Penguin Classics.

Harrison, Jane Ellen. (1991). *Prolegomena to the study of Greek religion*. Princeton University Press.

Heraclitus. (2001). *Fragments: The collected wisdom of Heraclitus* (Brooks Haxton, Trans.). Viking Adult.

Herman, Nini. (1989). *Too long a child: The mother-daughter dyad*. Free Association Books.

Hesiod. (1914). *Hesiod, the Homeric hymns, and Homerica*. Revised ed. Loeb Classical Library.

Hesse, Herman. (1971). *Siddhartha*. Bantam Books.

Hillman, James. (1975). *Re-Visioning psychology*. Harper & Row.

——(1979). *The dream and the underworld*. Harper & Row.

——(1996). *The soul's code: In search of character and calling*. Random House.

——(1997). *A blue fire*. (T. Moore, Ed.). HarperPerennial.

——(2004). *Archetypal psychology: Uniform edition of the writings of James Hillman, Vol. 1*. Third edition. Spring Publications.

——(2005). *Senex and puer: Uniform edition of the writings of James Hillman, Vol. 3*. (G. Slater, Ed.) Spring Publications.

——(2007). *Mythic Figures: Uniform edition of the writings of James Hillman,*
Vol. 6. Spring Publications.

——(2008). *Aphrodite's justice.* Edizioni La Conchiglia.

Hollister Wheelwright, Jane. (1984). *The power of the maiden.* Unpublished
lecture. Jane Hollister Wheelwright Manuscript Collection, Opus Archives
and Research Center.

Homer. (1990). *The Iliad* (R. Fagles, Trans.). Penguin Classics.

——(2018). *The Odyssey* (E. Wilson, Trans.). W. W. Norton & Company.

Hurwit, Jeffrey M. (1999). *The Athenian acropolis: History, mythology, and ar-*
chaeology from the Neolithic era to the present. Cambridge University Press.

Irigaray, Luce. (1993). *Je, tu, nous: Toward a culture of difference* (A. Martin,
Trans.). Routledge.

Jaffé, Aniela. (1984). *The myth of meaning in the work of C. G. Jung.* Daimon Verlag.

Johnson, Robert. (1976). *She: Understanding feminine psychology.* Harper & Row.

Jones, David. (2010). *The anathemata.* Faber & Faber.

Jung, C. G. (1967). *The collected works of C. G. Jung: Vol. 5. Symbols of transforma-*
tion (R. F. C. Hull, Trans.). (H. Read et al., Eds.). Princeton University Press.
(Original work published 1952)

——(1967). Commentary on "The secret of the golden flower" (R. F. C. Hull, Trans.).
(H. Read et al., Eds.). *The collected works of C. G. Jung: Vol. 13. Alchemical studies*
(pp. 1–56). Princeton University Press. (Original work published 1929)

——(1968). Concerning rebirth (R. F. C. Hull, Trans.). (H. Read et al., Eds.). *The*
collected works of C. G. Jung: Vol. 9 pt. 1. Archetypes and the collective un-
conscious (2nd ed., pp. 113–147). Princeton University Press. (Original work
published 1950)

——(1968). Individual dream symbolism in relation to alchemy (R. F. C. Hull,
Trans.). (H. Read et al., Eds.). *The collected works of C. G. Jung: Vol. 12.*
Psychology and alchemy (2nd ed., pp. 38–223). Princeton University Press.
(Original work published 1936)

——(1969). The psychological aspects of the Kore (R. F. C. Hull, Trans.). (H. Read
et al., Eds.). *The collected works of C. G. Jung: Vol. 9 pt. 1. Archetypes and the*
collective unconscious (2nd ed., pp. 182–203). Princeton University Press.
(Original work published 1951)

——(1969). Psychological aspects of the mother archetype (R. F. C. Hull, Trans.).
(H. Read et al., Eds.). *The collected works of C. G. Jung: Vol. 9 pt. 1. Archetypes*
and the collective unconscious (2nd ed., pp. 75–110). Princeton University
Press. (Original work published 1954)

——(1969). The psychology of the child archetype (R. F. C. Hull, Trans.). (H. Read et al., Eds.). *The collected works of C. G. Jung: Vol. 9 pt. 1. Archetypes and the collective unconscious* (2nd ed., pp. 151–181). Princeton University Press. (Original work published 1951)

——(1969). On the nature of the psyche (R. F. C. Hull, Trans.). (H. Read et al., Eds.). *The collected works of C. G. Jung: Vol. 8. Structure and dynamics of the psyche* (2nd ed., pp. 159–234). Princeton University Press. (Original work published 1954)

——(1969). Psychology and religion. (R. F. C. Hull, Trans.). (H. Read et al., Eds.). *The collected works of C. G. Jung: Vol. 11. Psychology and religion* (2nd ed., pp. 3-105). Princeton University Press. (Original work published 1940)

——(1997). *Visions: Notes of the seminar given in 1930–1934 by C.G. Jung.* C. Douglas (Ed.). Princeton University Press.

Jung, C. G., and Carl Kerényi. (1969). *Essays on a science of mythology: The myth of the divine child and the mysteries of Eleusis.* Princeton University Press.

Karakasi, Katerina. (2003). *Archaic korai.* J. Paul Getty Museum.

Kerényi, Karl. (1979). *Goddesses of sun and moon* (M. Stein, Trans.). Spring Publications.

——(1980). *The gods of the Greeks.* Reissue ed. Thames & Hudson.

——(1991). *Eleusis: Archetypal image of mother and daughter* (R. Manheim, Trans.). Princeton University Press.

Kingsford, Anna & Edward Maitland, Eds. And Trans.). (1885/2008). *Kore kosmou, or virgin of the world.* iUniverse.

Kinsley, David. (1988). *The goddesses' mirror: Visions of the divine from east and west.* SUNY Press.

Le Guin, Ursula. (1989). *Dancing at the edge of the world.* Harper & Row.

Leonard, Linda Schierse. (1982). *The wounded woman: Healing the father-daughter relationship.* Shambhala.

Levy, Ariel. (2018). *The rules do not apply: A memoir.* Random House.

Liddell, Henry George. (1925). *Greek-English lexicon.* Claredon Press.

Macko, Lia, and Kerry Rubin. (2005). *Midlife crisis at 30.* Plume.

MacLachlan, Bonnie. (1993). *The age of grace: Charis in early Greek poetry.* Princeton University Press.

Milani, Raffaelle. (2013). *The aesthetics of grace: Philosophy, art, and nature.* Peter Lang Inc., International Academic Publishers.

Mishan, Ligaya. (2020). Little Women. T: *The New York Times Style Magazine,* September 30.

Montgomery, L. M. (1982). *Anne of green gables*. Bantam Books.

Moore, Thomas. (1982). The virgin and the unicorn. In J. Stroud & G. Thomas (Eds.), *Images of the untouched: Virginity in psyche, myth and community*. (pp. 49–64). Dallas Institute for Humanities & Culture.

Mylonas, George E. (1961). *Eleusis and the Eleusinian mysteries*. Princeton University Press.

Neumann, Erich. (1974). *The great mother: An analysis of the archetype* (R. Manheim, Trans.). Princeton University Press.

O'Keeffe, Linda. (1996). *Shoes: A celebration of pumps, sandals, slippers & more*. Workman Publishing Company.

Orenstein, Peggy. (2001). *Flux: Women on sex, work, love, kids, and life in a half-changed world*. Anchor.

Otto, Walter. (1954). *The Homeric gods: The spiritual significance of Greek religion*. Pantheon Books.

Ovid. (1931). *Ovid: Fasti*. 2nd ed. (G. P. Goold, Ed.). Harvard University Press.

Ovid. (1993). *The metamorphoses of Ovid*. Houghton Mifflin Harcourt.

Paris, Ginette. (1986). *Pagan meditations: The worlds of Aphrodite, Artemis, and Hestia*. Spring Publications.

Pausanias. (1984). *Guide to Greece, Vol. 1: Central Greece* (P. Levi, Trans.). Penguin Classics.

Pindar. (1972). Odes of *Pindar I* (G. S. Conway, Trans.). Rowman & Littlefield.

Plato. (1996). *The republic: A new translation* (W. C. Scott, Trans.). W.W. Norton & Company.

Rayor, Diane J. (2014). *The Homeric hymns: A translation, with introduction and notes*. University of California Press.

Renault, Mary. (1988). *The king must die: A novel*. Vintage Books.

Rich, Adrienne. (2018). *Essential essays: Culture, politics, and the art of poetry*. W.W. Norton & Company.

Richter, Gisela. (1968). *Korai: Archaic Greek maidens*. Phaidon.

Ridgway, Brunilde. (1990). Birds, meniskoi, and head attributes in archaic Greece. *American Journal of Archaeology* 94: 583–612.

Rigoglioso, M. (2011). *The cult of divine birth in ancient Greece*. Palgrave Macmillan.

Rilke, R. M. (1990). *The Unknown Rilke* (F. Wright, Trans.). Oberlin College Press.

Sanford, John. (1995). *Fate, love, and ecstasy: Wisdom from the lesser-known goddesses of the Greeks*. Chiron Publications.

Sappho. (1986). *Sappho* (M. Barnard, Trans.). University of California Press.

Semmelhack, Elizabeth. (2017). *Shoes: The meaning of style.* Reaktion Books.

Shaw, Martin. (2014). *Snowy tower: Parzival and the wet black branch of language.* White Cloud Press.

Sissa, Giulia. (1990). *Greek virginity.* Harvard University Press.

Slaughter, Anne-Marie. (2012). Why women still can't have it all. *The Atlantic,* June 13 2012.

Smith, Betty M. (2008). The kore observed. *Psychological Perspectives* 47(2): 188–202.

Statista. 2020 July. *Footwear Report 2020.* https://www.statista.com/outlook/ 11000000/109/footwear/united-states.

Steele, Valerie, and Colleen Hill. (2013). *Shoe obsession.* Yale University Press.

Stieber, Mary. (2004). *The poetics of appearance in the attic korai.* University of Texas Press.

Szalai, Jennifer. (2017). The complicated origins of 'having it all.' *The New York Times,* December 21 2017.

Tait, Pamela. (2010). The kore: My experiences with the maiden archetype. *Psychological Perspectives* 53(2): 175–88.

Thomas, Dylan. (2017). *The poems of Dylan Thomas.* New Directions.

Tippet, Krista. (2016). Hindu saying as quoted in Sharon Salzberg's 'cupping our hands to grace.' *On Being.* Retrieved January 20, 2016

Turner, Ralph V. (2011). *Eleanor of Aquitaine: Queen of France, queen of England.* Yale University Press.

Ulanov, Ann Belford. (1971). *The feminine in Jungian psychology and in Christian theology.* Northwestern University Press.

Von Franz, Marie-Louse. (1993). *The feminine in fairy tales.* Revised ed. Shambhala.

Weir, Alison. (2001). *Eleanor of Aquitaine.* 2nd ed. Ballantine Books.

Wheeler, B., John C. Parsons, and Elizabeth Brown, eds. (2008). *Eleanor of Aquitaine: Lord and lady.* Palgrave Macmillan.

Wiktionary. (17 November 2020). *Reconstruction:Proto-Indo-European/dʰugh₂tḗr.* https://en.wiktionary.org/wiki/Reconstruction:Proto-Indo-European/d% CA%Bough%E2%82%82t%E1%B8%97r.

Wind, Edgar. (1969). *Pagan mysteries in the Renaissance.* Revised ed. W.W. Norton & Company.

Woodman, Marion. (1982). *Addiction to perfection.* Inner City Books.

——(1985). *The pregnant virgin: A process of psychological transformation.* Inner City Books.

Woodman, Marion and Marlene Schiwy. (2011). *Marion Woodman DVD series.* Schiwy Films.

Woodman, Marion, and Elinor Dickson. (1997). *Dancing in the flames: The dark goddess in the transformation of consciousness.* Shambhala.

Yeats, W. B. (1994). *The Collected Poems of W. B. Yeats.* Wordsworth Editions Limited.

Yousafzai, Malala, and Patricia McCormick. (2014). *I am Malala: How one girl stood up for education and changed the world (Young Readers Edition).* Little, Brown and Co.

Zuntz, Günther. (1971). *Persephone: Three essays on religion and thought in magna Graecia.* Clarendon Press.

Made in the USA
Las Vegas, NV
28 January 2022

42482348R00118